"Your Own Prof~~~~~~~~~~~ In 72 Hours... (or Less!)"

www

Jim Edwards'

"How To Make Your Own Outrageously Profitable Info-Products In 72 Hours... (or Less!)"

© MMX – JIM EDWARDS. All rights reserved.

Jim Edwards – www.TheNetReporter.com/fasttrack

What People Are Saying About Jim Edwards and

"How To Make Your Own Outrageously Profitable Info-Products In 72 Hours... (or Less!)"...

"Getting a product together in 72 hours is really a piece of cake if you follow Jim's simple plan."

    -Lowell Bascom

"You convinced me that you can research a market, and create a product in 72 hours or less, including what to charge, how to "chunk" it and put it together, where to find experts and resources, and you included not just one, but FOUR different MARKET BLUEPRINTS.

The only thing we have to do is follow the blueprint to creating a successful product FAST!"

    -Patty Rutkowski

"I liked the 4 steps and 72 hours to an internet product you outlined..

It was packed with many pearls of wisdom highly concentrated in such a short time taken from those years of hands-on experience; beautifully done Jim, thanks.

I especially liked the direction on using the webinar format if your niche is in solution(s) to a problem that won't go away. Good one, I never thought of it like that before.."

    -Robert Doktor

"If you want to create a down and dirty, useful info product... follow Jim's info step by step."

-Patti Malone

"Jim laid out the foundation to create an info product in less than 3 days.... no more time excuses for not creating product!"

-Jeremy Fleming

"... the best I have seen on getting started with my own info product. The time for excuses is past. Jim has laid out a clear path to follow and for me its time to get it done."

-Charles Looper

"I liked the frank discussion of price points and specifics of how to produce a product in 72 hours or less. Needed this to get my act in gear and add to my product line. Thanks Jim!"

-Máire Clements

"... The best of it all, though, was the step-by-step walkthrough on how to go from start to finish on creating an info-product in 72 hours."

-Jeff Baas

"Jim has again reduced the complex to a series of simple steps including resources that will enable the newest marketer to get a quality product together and produced in a weekend."

-Michael Gormley

Limits of Liability / Disclaimer of Warranty:

The authors and publisher of this book and the accompanying materials have used their best efforts in preparing this program. The authors and publisher make no representation or warranties with respect to the accuracy, applicability, fitness, or completeness of the contents of this program for any purpose. They disclaim any warranties (expressed or implied), merchantability, or fitness for any particular purpose. The authors and publisher shall in no event be held liable for any loss or other damages, including but not limited to special, incidental, consequential, or other damages. As always, the advice of a competent legal, tax, accounting or other professional should be sought. The authors and publisher don't warrant the performance, effectiveness or applicability of any sites or resources listed in this book. All links and resources are for information purposes only and are not warranted for content, accuracy or any other implied or explicit purpose.

This manual contains material protected under International and Federal Copyright Laws and Treaties. Any unauthorized reprint or use of this material is prohibited.

Copyright Information

Copyright © 2010 by Jim Edwards

All Rights Reserved. No part of this book may be used or reproduced in any manner whatsoever without prior written consent of the author, except as provided by the United States of America copyright law.

Published by **AQuickReadBook**.com™
A Division of Guaranteed Response Marketing, LLC

A Quick Read Book™ is a Trademark of Guaranteed Response Marketing, LLC

Printed in the United States of America

ISBN: See back cover

Most **AQuickReadBook.com** titles are available at special quantity discounts for bulk purchases for sales promotions, premiums, fundraising, gifts or educational use. Also, special customized / company specific versions or excerpts can be created to fit specific needs.

For more information, please contact us at A Quick Read Book™ online at www.AQuickReadBook.com

"Your Own Profitable Info-Products In 72 Hours... (or Less!)"

What is A Quick Read Book™?

A Quick Read Book™ helps authors and readers connect much faster than with a traditional book.

FACT: We live in a fast-paced, "need-it-now" society.

FACT: Traditional books contain 20% content, and 80% "extra" that just fills up pages to add "bulk".

FACT: People don't have time to waste, especially when it comes to solving pressing issues and problems in their business or personal lives.

A Quick Read Book™ solves all those problems, and much, MUCH more!

As a reader, you get to cut straight to the heart of a book's contents, without wading through hundreds of extra pages of fluff. You get exactly what you need to succeed with the author's topic, and none of the extra filler.

As an author, you get to share the exact facts, tips, tricks and insider information your audience needs to succeed. And you don't have the pressure from a traditional publisher that just wants to fill pages with unnecessary text.

For more **A Quick Read Book™** titles and information about becoming **A Quick Read Book™** author, please visit us at the **www.AQuickReadBook.com**™ publisher's website today.

Visit Us Online

www.AQuickReadBook.com™

At the **A Quick Read Book**™ website, you'll find:

Chapter Excerpts from selected New Releases

•

Original Author and Editor Articles

•

Audio Excerpts

•

Electronic Newsletters

•

Author Contact Information

•

Tools and Resources Center

•

Plus Much, MUCH More!

•

Bookmark the **A Quick Read Book**™ Website at **www.AQuickReadBook.com**™

Meet Your Author

About Jim Edwards

Jim Edwards, founder of Guaranteed Response Marketing,LLC, is an Internet expert, marketing entrepreneur, newspaper columnist, author, motivational speaker and elite mentor and coach.

Having gained personal and financial freedom for himself and his family, he shares his proven strategies with self-motivated, hard-working people to help them attain personal and financial independence.

He has written and published dozens of ebooks, print books and hundreds of articles. Through his company, Jim has produced some 30 informational products on DVD and many more available in the latest electronic formats downloadable from the Internet. Jim produces and hosts webinars on a weekly basis and has been a frequent guest speaker at numerous international Internet marketing seminars.

He offers the exclusive "Jim Boat" seminar, an intensive seven-day program integrated into a Caribbean cruise, an inspirational setting for focusing on ways to achieve success. In its third year, the 2009 Jim Boat included over 100 participants from six countries.

Jim's successes are most compelling because they stem from his true life story. From childhood Jim was always driven to succeed. Though he excelled as a young man in real estate and mortgage banking, Jim left the industry to launch his own business.

In just a few short years, his business failed, he lost all he acquired, and he struggled to support his family and survive.

He developed a heart condition and landed in the hospital staring death in the face. Thereafter, he declared bankruptcy.

With only one way to go, Jim climbed his way up, up and up using his keen mastery of the Internet, a simple marketing strategy and hard, honest work.

Within two years he was financially stable and free.

A prolific creator and writer, Jim constantly has several books and new products in development at any given time.

What motivates him most is seeing how his work helps others free themselves of the shackles of financial servitude to the corporate world. His goal is to help self-motivated smart, hard-workers liberate themselves from the corporate establishment to build their own business and attain personal freedom.

"Your Own Profitable Info-Products In 72 Hours... (or Less!)"

He has been featured in Entrepreneur magazine, and his products have ranked number one best selling in the educational, business and economics and special interest, business categories on Amazon.

His latest works include *The Net Reporter*, *True Life Success Lessons* and the wildly successful *I Gotta Tell You* blog and newsletter.

Find out more about Jim's latest projects here:

Jim's SPECIAL OFFER

The Net Reporter
"Fast Track Video Coaching"

You get access to Jim's 6-Module "Fast Track Video Coaching" sessions that will take you Step-By-Step from ZERO to your own crazy profitable online business faster than you ever dreamed possible- a $997 Value - FREE!

Get all the details here:

www.TheNetReporter.com/ftvc

For Terri,
who always believed in me, even when I didn't.

For little Johnny,
who showed me the meaning of unconditional love.

For my parents, Pat & Dallas…
see, all that talking when I was a little kid
finally paid off!

"Your Own Profitable Info-Products In 72 Hours... (or Less!)"

Table of Contents

What is **A Quick Read Book**™? 7

Meet Your Author 9

What We'll Cover... 17

Entry Level Products Vs. Niche-Committed Level Products.......21

Pricing in the "Real" World 27

Typical Product Blueprints 33

Blueprint #1 – Step-By-Step 35

Blueprint #2 – Quick-Start Guide 43

Blueprint #3 – Lots of Problems..49

Blueprint #4 – Ongoing Problems 57

The Fastest Products You Can Create 65

Twitter Inspiration 73

Step-By-Step What I'd Specifically Do, If I Only Had 48 to 72 Hours to Create a Unique Product...77

Day 1 – Compile Questions 79

Day 2 – Ask & Answer 85

Day 3 – Add The Trimmings 89

Final Thoughts...97

Bulk Book Order & Customized Version Information 99

More Help From Jim Edwards...101

What We'll Cover...

Welcome!

Today we're going to cover *How To Create A Killer Info Product At A Profitable Price Point Fast: How You Can Conceptualize And Develop A Kick-Ass, Unique Info Product In 72 Hours Or Less*.

What I'm finding is that, when it comes to product creation, if it doesn't happen fast, it's not going to happen at all. Something that takes three weeks or a month to do, most people give up and move on to something else.

Real quick, here are the results of an audience poll I did with everybody at a live presentation.

> Do you currently have a product selling online, making you money?

- Yes, I have more than three.

- Yes, I have one and I'm doing okay.

- Yes, but it's not making me any money.

- No, but I sure want one.

I want to see where everybody is relative to everybody else so that we can make sure we address everybody's needs.

These are the results:

7% - Yes, I have more than three.

16% - Yes, I have one and I'm doing okay.

21% - Yes, but it's not making me any money.

57% - No, but I sure want one.

I would tell you this, for those in the top two categories.

This is going to help you to really understand the main categories that info products fall into. It's then going to show you how you could maybe even modify your current approach, but definitely how you could add another product really fast to your stable.

For those of you, I guess about 78% that have one but it's not making you any money. Or you don't have one at all, this is kind of a great way for you to start from scratch the right way.

Make sure that you have your pricing, as well as how you're positioning your product, as well as the actual product that you create in good shape right out of the gate.

With no further ado, let's go ahead and get into the presentation.

What are we going to cover?

We're going to go over:

"Your Own Profitable Info-Products In 72 Hours... (or Less!)"

- Test/Entry Level Products Vs. Niche-Committed Level Products

- Pricing In The "Real" World

- Typical Product Blueprints

- Four Specific Product Patterns You Can Use

- WWJD: What Would Jim Do For Each One Of These

- Step-By-Step What I'd Specifically Do If I Only Had 48 To 72 Hours To Create A Unique Product

And, of course, Much, MUCH More!

Let's go over info product categories, your objectives, and real world pricing.

This is going to give you a quick thumbnail to just kind of make sure everybody's on the same page.

Test/Entry Level Products Vs. Niche-Committed Level Products

Really, info products, as far as I'm concerned, fall into one of these five categories. Sometimes, the easiest thing to do is to look at things in terms of asking questions. You're asking questions to help evaluate really, really fast your target audience.

As I go through these real fast, which one of these best describes your target audience?

Just think about it.

What is the single biggest category where you see the people that you're targeting, falling into?

- Do they need step-by step help?

- Do thy have trouble getting started or knowing where to start?

This is, by the way, a great type of product to make if you're relatively new to a niche. You can make your money by helping other people get their start.

- Do they have a very specific problem that needs solving?

- Do they have lots of little annoying problems?

It's not one thing. It's a whole bunch of things that they need to take care of.

- Do they have ongoing problems?

In other words, once they solve one problem, do they earn the right to solve another?

Your answer to this really dictates the type of product that you're going to create. We're going to talk about each one in just a few minutes.

I just wanted to show you that these are the categories that I look at when I'm looking to create a product.

These apply whether it's in a new niche or a niche that I'm already in for an audience that I know or understand, or I'm trying to know and understand.

I'm always thinking in terms of:

- "Do they need some sort of step-by-step?

- Are they having trouble even getting started?

- Do they have a very specific problem that they need to solve?

- Are there lots of little annoying problems, or are there ongoing problems?"

"Your Own Profitable Info-Products In 72 Hours... (or Less!)"

Again, the answer to that question most appropriate to your niche is going to dictate the type of product that you're going to create.

Aside from the categories, we also need to look at **your objectives in creating an information product**.

No matter what niche you're in, you really have two levels that you're going to be looking at in creating a product.

Look where you are, in relation to building your business in the niche. Are you established or are you just getting started and need to move quickly to see if this is where you're actually going to "make your stand."

This is going to determine whether you come out with a home-study course or just a special report, a smaller ebook.

Also it applies whether you do a six CD or six DVD course versus a couple of CDs, if you're trying to go and do a physical course.

You need to ask yourself, "Am I just testing out this market? Do I need an entry level product, or do I need a niche-committed level product?"

If the answer is the first one, if you need a test/entry level product, then really the purpose of this product is not to get rich. The purpose of this product is to test for signs of life.

This is where you're going to see if you can make a connection with a niche market.

This is also where you could do a hit and run on a market.

If you're one of those people that wants to do multiple niches but none of them too deeply, then you need to be able to knock out a product that has a high-perceived value.

It really narrows in with a laser focus on exactly the problem or the category of info product that that niche needs. You need to be able to do it really, really fast.

On the flip side, the other type of product you could do is a "niche-committed level" product. That's basically a market you want to build out. You've tested this market, and you feel strongly that it can pan out for you.

This is going to be a product that is going to have a higher perceived level of value, but it doesn't necessarily have to take any longer than creating a test/entry level product.

You might say, "How could you do that?"

A little later on in the webinar, I'm going to show you exactly how you do that.

This type of product is usually either more in depth, or specialized in one area.

This probably would not be a quick-start guide.

This would be more along the lines of something where they have one really specific problem that's bugging the heck out of them. They really want to solve it in a big, big way.

"Your Own Profitable Info-Products In 72 Hours... (or Less!)"

This would be something where you would have a bigger, more committed level of product.

Jim's SPECIAL OFFER

The Net Reporter
"Fast Track Video Coaching"

You get access to Jim's 6-Module "Fast Track Video Coaching" sessions that will take you Step-By-Step from ZERO to your own crazy profitable online business faster than you ever dreamed possible- a $997 Value - FREE!

* Module 1: Mindset & Niche Market Research
* Module 2: Getting your Web Presence up fast
* Module 3: Your Sales Message
* Module 4: Your Own High-Value Product
* Module 5: Fast Targeted Traffic
* Module 6: List Building

Get all the details here:

www.TheNetReporter.com/ftvc

Pricing in the "Real" World

Let's talk for a minute about pricing in the real world, because I'm going to be honest with you. We need to talk a little bit about real niche marketing reality versus Internet marketing fantasy.

There are a lot of people in the Internet marketing world who will say, "You write your own ticket. You're selling stuff too cheap. There's no reason why you can't sell something in this little niche market for $100, $200. You've got stinkin' thinking,' and on and on and on."

That's a load of bull.

There is a reality.

There is Internet marketing reality, and then there is the reality of the real world and how people spend money. What they think is the right price for something.

When you're looking at entry level info products in the real world, consumers are going to pay between $19 and $49 for some sort of information product without breathing too hard.

A quick way to know this is to go and look at sites like ClickBank.com's Marketplace, like Amazon.

This is like going out on the web and just doing a search like you were in a niche market. See what's actually out there that's available.

You will see that in the consumer market, an entry level product would be a book, an ebook, DVD, CD, maybe a home-study course.

Another place that you could go look is someplace like Nightingale Conan. You'll see a lot of their stuff, they run specials and things like that. You can get a six CD set from them, in a lot of cases, under $49, especially if they're selling MP3s.

If it's a make-money topic, then typically, in the real world, that's going to cost somewhere between $29 and $99. We're talking about entry level products. We're talking about the first product that you're going to offer somebody.

You've run some traffic to your website. They show up. They don't know you from Adam. They're going to spend somewhere between $19 and $100, depending on what you're selling, what the promise is, how good the positioning is.

I don't care how good the promise is, how good the positioning is. You're probably, in the vast majority of cases, never going to get more than $100 out of somebody for an entry level product.

I define an entry level product as a DVD, a couple of CDs, a book, an ebook, special report.

Pricing in the "Real" World

Let's talk for a minute about pricing in the real world, because I'm going to be honest with you. We need to talk a little bit about real niche marketing reality versus Internet marketing fantasy.

There are a lot of people in the Internet marketing world who will say, "You write your own ticket. You're selling stuff too cheap. There's no reason why you can't sell something in this little niche market for $100, $200. You've got stinkin' thinking,' and on and on and on."

That's a load of bull.

There is a reality.

There is Internet marketing reality, and then there is the reality of the real world and how people spend money. What they think is the right price for something.

When you're looking at entry level info products in the real world, consumers are going to pay between $19 and $49 for some sort of information product without breathing too hard.

A quick way to know this is to go and look at sites like ClickBank.com's Marketplace, like Amazon.

This is like going out on the web and just doing a search like you were in a niche market. See what's actually out there that's available.

You will see that in the consumer market, an entry level product would be a book, an ebook, DVD, CD, maybe a home-study course.

Another place that you could go look is someplace like Nightingale Conan. You'll see a lot of their stuff, they run specials and things like that. You can get a six CD set from them, in a lot of cases, under $49, especially if they're selling MP3s.

If it's a make-money topic, then typically, in the real world, that's going to cost somewhere between $29 and $99. We're talking about entry level products. We're talking about the first product that you're going to offer somebody.

You've run some traffic to your website. They show up. They don't know you from Adam. They're going to spend somewhere between $19 and $100, depending on what you're selling, what the promise is, how good the positioning is.

I don't care how good the promise is, how good the positioning is. You're probably, in the vast majority of cases, never going to get more than $100 out of somebody for an entry level product.

I define an entry level product as a DVD, a couple of CDs, a book, an ebook, special report.

"Your Own Profitable Info-Products In 72 Hours... (or Less!)"

The thing is you can step it up from there, once you have a customer. Again, it is a proven fact that someone who buys something from you once, is likely to buy something from you again. They are at least more likely to buy from you again, than trying to get somebody to buy in the first place.

As far as pricing in the real world, the first part is pricing it in a range that they expect, so price is not the issue.

Where you want them considering, and I've heard people say this before, "Oh, price is never the issue. It's the value. Your price is never too high. Your perceived value is too low."

Yes, that's true to an extent. But there does reach a point where somebody says, "I ain't paying $59 for 1 DVD or for 1 audio CD."

There's a point where you'll get some people who will pay it, but the vast majority will say, "I'm just not paying $59 for 1 single CD."

Once you have them as a customer, then you can start working them over. They don't have as much to compare. They're not comparing you to someone else. They know you. They've bought from you. They like you. They trust you.

Now, they're just making an evaluation, "Hey. Do I want this for $97, $197, $597?"

You have to get them as a customer first.

Pricing is more than just worrying about the price on the front end of the info product that you're going to sell them. Pricing in the real world also means that you diversify your offers.

This is where you actually make the real money without trying to make each product a homerun. That's what a lot of these Internet marketing courses try to teach you. "You're going to hit your homerun with this particular course."

My business was built on bunts and singles and doubles, with an occasional homerun put in there. Really, that's the difference between running a business and having a one-time promotion.

Pricing means that in the same niche, you have upsells, you have back end offers and you have continuity offers. Also in related niches, you make multiple offers within similar niches.

If it works in this niche, if there's a similar niche, then maybe you can take what you have in this niche and make that same offer in a related niche.

A good example of that might be campers versus hikers, people who are really into camping versus people who are really into hiking. Those are very related niches, and you might be able to sell similar stuff to them.

You do this for upsells, to have back end offers, once you have a product out there that's selling. I don't care who you are, and I'm talking as much to myself, you must have an upsell. You have to have back end offers.

I've always been great on back end offers and continuity offers now, continuity for the last three years. But I've never been that good with upsells. I need to get more proficient at that, and so I'm taking steps to do that.

The thing is to do this. You need a way to come up with the right product at the right price, in a really short period of time instead of spending six months to develop a product your audience might be interested in.

It would be much better if you have a product that's selling, and even if it's just breaking even. I had a guy who was in a coaching class of mine. We helped him put together an offer. It was actually a dog training-related offer.

Right out of the gate, from day one, with cold AdWords traffic and not really any research, he was breaking even. For every $50 he was spending on AdWords, he was bringing in $49, $50, $51.

He starts bitching to me that he's only breaking even, and he's getting tired of breaking even. I said, "Let's do an upsell."

For whatever reason, he wouldn't do an upsell. I think he just ran into a brick wall for whatever reason.

We took that product from him, I bought it from him, and we added an upsell.

Instantly, you have profitability.

The thing is you must have a strategy for being able to create a product really, really fast.

In order to do that, you really have to have a blueprint that you're going to follow, and a method for creating the content quickly.

Typical Product Blueprints

Let's talk about typical info product blueprints. In fact, we have four specific info product patterns that you can use.

I have on each one of them an evaluation criteria to kind of breakdown each blueprint.

We're going to talk about the promise, which is basically, "What's the promise of the product relative to the other types of products out there?"

We're going to talk about the product type. I'm going to talk about the type of product that I'd recommend that you create. Everybody wants to know, "Okay, Jim. What would you do?"

Then we're going to talk about price points for each one. I'm going to talk about real world pricing, not Internet marketing fantasy land.

Finally, what would Jim do? What if I only had 48 to 72 hours to create a product? What would I do?

I have to tell you. I would not sit down and write an ebook on any of these. That may come as a surprise, because back in 1997 to 2002, that's exactly what I would've told you to do. Sit down, write an ebook. You need to sit down and write an ebook.

In February of 2003, I was exposed to online multimedia, audio products, recording, things like that.

A whole new world opened up for me. I'm not saying that ebooks don't work. In fact, I'm going to show you how to create an ebook in 3 days here, in a little while… you just don't want to write it out word for word.

Let's just jump right in.

Blueprint #1 – Step-By-Step

The first blueprint is, a specific problem needs solving, step-by-step.

This is really the easiest one to do. It's also the easiest one to sell, because of the promise to the consumer or to the business owner, or whoever's in your niche target audience. The promise is real simple.

It's real straightforward.

"I'll teach you step-by-step, how to go from where you are now, to where you want to be."

Think about it from the standpoint of they're over there and they want to be over here, and there's this gap. **You're going to show them how to bridge the gap.**

You only need to be a very basic level copywriter to be able to explain that to somebody.

This is one of the easiest things that you can do, especially when you get down into a niche market where it's just real simple. You want to know how to do this. I'm going to show you how to do this step-by-step-by-step.

What product type should you create when you're thinking about creating some sort of a step-by-step product?

Number one, if you're doing anything computer-related, do something with software, something to do with anything that you can show on the computer screen.

If you've watched any of my webinars, we've shown a lot of things on the computer screen that really didn't have anything to do with actual computer stuff.

If you can use PowerPoint, then you can use screen capture video to teach anyone step-by-step how to do virtually anything.

Just as an aside look in my membership www.thenetreporter.com. You have a world class education on how to use screen capture video to create your own, what I call ,"multimedia info product."

There is a complete course that really should cost a couple of thousand dollars that you can gain access to right there in the membership site.
,
There are a lot of things that you can do with screen capture video, and it's a way to create high value content really, really fast.

Another type of product you can do step-by-step, whatever problem needs solving, you can use full motion video. That's really best for something that happens in the real world.

It's anything that you could show somebody, step-by-step, how to do, everything from tying your shoe to arts and crafts, to fixing your car to restoring your antique furniture.

"Your Own Profitable Info-Products In 72 Hours... (or Less!)"

Whatever it is, if you can do full motion video of it, then you can turn that into a product.

Also in *The Net Reporter*, we have a ton of information to teach you specifically how to do full motion video.

Audio really works when you don't need a visual to explain something. Can you just explain something to somebody?

A great way to figure out whether you could do that or not is to ask, "Could this be explained to somebody over the phone. Whether it is through a conference call, or could I call somebody and explain this? Or could I call someone who knows the steps, knows step-by-step how to solve this problem. **Could I call them and have them explain it to me over the phone?**"

If the answer is **yes**, then you can just do some sort of an audio product.

Price points, what can you charge for a step-by-step tutorial or step-by-step instructions on how to do something from point A to point Z?

This one is probably the widest range of prices, because it really comes down to what is it worth to you to learn this? That is also, by the way, a great phrase to use in your sales copy.

"What's it worth to you to learn how to do this, to not have the pain of not knowing how to do it? What's it worth to you to have somebody show you step-by-step how to go from where you are right now, to exactly where you want to be?"

Again, an entry level product, I'm not talking about a home-study course. I'm not talking about 12 DVDs. I'm not talking about, really in this case, 6 or 8 audio CDs.

I'm just talking about an ebook or a couple of audio CDs, or a single DVD.

If it's a consumer-related topic, you're going to get $50 and under. It might be $19. It might be $29.

The easiest way to figure it out is go look at what they're paying for either similar stuff, or what your target audience is paying for books, CDs, DVDs?

What are the typical price points out there, plus or minus 10%, that's pretty much what you're going to get on an entry level info product.

If it's a business-related topic, the price point is somewhere between $97 and $197. I put $197 and under.

The high end is really going to be around $197, and $29 to $49 on the lower end.

That's going to depend also on the bulk of the information.

If it's a single DVD, it's hard to get $100 for a single DVD.

But could you take the information on that single DVD and put it onto 2 DVDs?

"Your Own Profitable Info-Products In 72 Hours... (or Less!)"

It's still an entry level product, but it feels like it has more to it. It feels like it has more value.

The next question is, "What would Jim do in this situation." I ask myself the question, **"If I only had 72 hours to create a step-by-step info product," this is what I would do.**

I would create a series of screen capture videos to teach people how to do something on their computer, that a lot of people want to know how to do. It would either be computer-related or it would be software-related.

That's just me.

I've made my living now for the last 13+ years teaching people how to do stuff on their computer, with their computer. That's been a big component of what I'm doing.

I would do some research, and I would figure out what the target audience really wanted to know, that involved using their computer or using software.

If there wasn't something computer-related or software-related, then I would figure out a way to use multimedia to create a multimedia info product to sell them.

I would also try to tie in a make-money aspect if possible. You're thinking, "Oh, you're just going to make a make-money product."

You can pretty much turn any product into either a make-money product or at least put a make-money spin on that product.

You can tell them, "Look. You can do it for yourself so you're going to save this money over hiring someone else, and this has the potential, I'm not telling you 100% that you could. But if you get really good at this, you might be able to do this for other people and charge them."

That's a basic make-money spin that you can put on a ton of stuff. Just by saying, "Once you get this done, you could turn around and do it for other people and charge them."

Another angle that you can put on a product is to tell them, "Hey, look. I designed this to teach you step-by-step how to do it. But even if you don't want to know how to do it, you at least could take this and hand it to someone in your organization".

This works well with business-related stuff, "hand this to someone in your organization, and here's your training in a box. Here's how to teach somebody how to do this for you."

That's another great line of copy that you can use to help move a product.

You could also do, what I would also consider doing instead of just creating a series of screen capture videos. You could also do a webinar or a webinar series. You see me doing that a lot now, because that's a way that I can create high-value content for, in some cases, thousands of people in a very short period of time.

That's why they call me the "Webinar King."
I'm only that good because I've been doing it and doing it, over and over again.

What I would certainly do then is have everything transcribed. Then I would add screen shots so that I could offer the multimedia and the printed manual without writing anything.

That's a biggie. That's one of the big things that I have figured out over the last few years. If you record it, get it transcribed. If you want to add more value to it, add screen shots of whatever you're talking about. All of a sudden, that takes a transcript.

A lot of people do transcripts of teleseminars and things like that, but it just seems like it's raw text.

You should know that just by adding simple screen shots to some sort of transcript, whether it's from a teleseminar or having your screen capture videos transcribed, it massively increases the perceived value without really increasing the workload very much at all.

A variation on the step-by-step problem, instead of a step-by-step problem, it could be **a series of problems in a sequence**.

I like to think of it like dominoes that you teach them to line up and knock down.

A great example of this in my own business was, and is, the *33 Days to Online Profits* video set.

Basically, what Yanik Silver and I did was take the 20% of the *33 Days to Online Profits* ebook that made the 80% impact, and we taught how to do that using video.

Instead of trying to teach them everything, we taught them the most high impact information using video.

The great thing is we made that in two days.

We made that in a weekend.

Literally, we took an ebook and we turned it into a video product, in a very, very short period of time.

What *33 Days to Online Profits* does is show you how to eliminate a series of problems in a sequence. You could just as easily do "33 Days to," or "14 Steps to," or "15 Days to" whatever. It's just a series of problems that somebody has to solve.

They're just problems or steps, or whatever you want to call them.

"Your Own Profitable Info-Products In 72 Hours... (or Less!)"

Blueprint #2 – Quick-Start Guide

The second blueprint is a blueprint for a product where they're basically having trouble getting started, or trouble knowing where to start, or they need a quick-start guide.

If you're looking for niches where there's a need for something a quick-start guide, where do I get started, things like? You need look no further than the *Dummies* books or the *Idiots* books. Those are really the ultimate quick-start guides for just about anything.

The promise of a quick-start guide is primarily a basic training or a boot camp or a fast start for a specific problem that people have, and they don't know how to get started with it.

Your promise is to give very clearly defined objectives for what they should expect. It's very black and white. Usually, it's a single strong promise, something like, "If you're not sure how to get started building your first business website, this is for you."

"If you have no clue how to get started making your child behave and listen, then this is for you."

It's real straightforward, and it's usually very, very strong.

This is aimed at people who are ignorant, know they're ignorant, and don't want to be ignorant anymore. They are eager for someone to take them by the hand, and explain the basics.

The one negative, if you know anything about the topic, you can often brush past things that people think are really important. This is why it's important to do really good research, and understand the things they're really going to face when they're first starting out, and to limit the scope.

That's another thing that you have to be really careful of, you don't give them too much.

One real strong promise, you're going to get this, this, this, and this, and this is how you're going to get going. It's not going to have all the advanced stuff. That's for the next course.

The product types that you really want to think about doing, some sort of audio or video product is always going to be the fastest.

But you can also add a ton of value to any quick-start guide by having some sort of step-by-step PDF report with lots of screen shots and diagrams, also checklists of steps.

If you go down to your book store or the office supply store, you probably see or have seen these laminated guides. Sometimes, they are a single sheet front and back.

A lot of them are shortcuts for things like Word, PowerPoint, Excel.

"Your Own Profitable Info-Products In 72 Hours... (or Less!)"

I have bought them before on how to play Blackjack, how to play Texas Hold 'Em. They're everything boiled down. They're almost like a mind map. If you were to do a mind map of the 30 most important things that someone should know starting from scratch in this market, what should they know?

That's actually a great question where you ask somebody to do some research for you.

What are the 30 biggest things that someone should know, or the 30 tips or the 30 nuggets that someone should know, when they're first starting out in a niche market?

They just go onto either a checklist, or some sort of laminated guide.

What you can also do to increase value is just use a combination of the three. You have an audio CD or a video DVD, and you also have a downloadable report or a printed book.

I would probably do the downloadable report because then they have to give you their name and email.

Add some sort of a checklist or guide, a print and post, come up with some catchy name for it, print and post cheat sheet. That's another thing you can call step two, a cheat sheet. A cheat sheet will get everybody's attention.

You have a great product there. You have a ton of value, "perceived" value just by adding something with some screen shots, and then a list of resources and things like that.

Typically for a quick-start guide, your price points are going to be a little bit lower. For a consumer, you're looking at $19 to $39.

If you had just one of those checklists by itself, I bought those laminated checklists before for $4.99, $5.99, $6.99.

I have absolutely zero interest in trying to sell something for $5.99 on the Internet. You have to mix and match things together to come up with enough value, so you can get that price up to $20, $30, $40.

In the business make-money category, you're still looking somewhere between $19 and $99, entry level, a quick-start type guide.

Are there exceptions to this rule? Sure, there are quick-start type guides out there that sell for a couple of thousand dollars, but that's a home-study course.

That's not a hit and run, a quick end of the market, a see if I can sell, see if I can establish a beachhead, or as it were, with a particular market.

Frankly, you're probably not going to stick around long enough to create a quick-start guide/home-study course if you don't already have a list. You don't already have distribution, and somebody to help you sell the thing. You're just not going to do it.

"Your Own Profitable Info-Products In 72 Hours... (or Less!)"

By structuring it this way, you have a higher chance of actually succeeding.

What would I do if I only had 72 hours to create a quick-start guide? I would do a webinar or a GoToMeeting, with a very clearly defined objective and promise. I would show people exactly how to get started on whatever topic it was.

I'm going to share with you in a minute, how I would do that, even if I didn't know a darn thing about the topic.

One thing I will tell you, though, and just burn this into your brain because it's actually really simple.

If it's an info-related topic, in other words the quick-start guide is merely just laying stuff out for them. Let's say I was doing a quick-start guide for the top 15 things that your company should know about hazardous materials.

"If you ship hazardous materials, here are the 15 things every employee should know."

I would just do a PowerPoint. I would do a very PowerPoint-intensive presentation.

If it was a how-to related topic, then I would use some sort of screen action teaching, especially if it was teaching somebody how to do something with or on their computer.

Then I'd just show them how to do it with or on their computer.

Jim's SPECIAL OFFER

The Net Reporter
"Fast Track Video Coaching"

You get access to Jim's 6-Module "Fast Track Video Coaching" sessions that will take you Step-By-Step from ZERO to your own crazy profitable online business faster than you ever dreamed possible- a $997 Value - FREE!

Get all the details here:

www.TheNetReporter.com/ftvc

"Your Own Profitable Info-Products In 72 Hours... (or Less!)"

Blueprint #3 – Lots of Problems

The third blueprint is one that you're going to see in a lot of niches, where there are lots of little annoying problems.

A good one I'm familiar with is web masters.

There are a bunch of different things that someone might want to know about FrontPage. Even though FrontPage isn't even being made anymore, there are still a ton of people out there using it. Also, Dreamweaver is another one.

There are a ton of little things that you want to know how to do, but there is no single problem big enough to stand alone as the product. Instead there are a ton of little problems, so then you just knock those out.

The promise of this type of product is basically, "This product will give you a solid education, and turn you into an expert in a specific area."

Also, "It promises to give you a large amount of information in a very short period of time."

The great thing about these is writing the sales letter for an info product that solves a bunch of little problems. It is actually really, really easy.

Each one of those problems becomes either a bullet or a paragraph, where you just tell them, "Hey. We're going to teach you how to deal with tables, and solve that issue once and for all."

I'm speaking to the web master issue now.

"We're going to teach you how to position graphics, how to sample graphics, how to resample graphics, and create screen resolution in graphics that are small, lightweight, and load really fast. But they look terrific no matter what type of browser people are using."

You knock out each one of those little problems. The sales copy writes itself.

A lot of times, people will buy the product because of just one of the little problems that you solve.

But they have to buy the whole product, and they feel good that there is other information there for them as well.

Again, audio or video is absolutely the fastest. One thing I will tell you is make sure you use the chunk format. That means each problem has its own chunk, its own chapter, its own video, its on section in the video.

If you watch how I do these presentations, a lot of these presentations, they're divided up into chunks. Right now, we're on the third blueprint, but each one of those blueprints is clearly delineated by a title screen.

It's its own little chunk.

"Your Own Profitable Info-Products In 72 Hours... (or Less!)"

You can do the same thing when you're solving each one of these problems for people. It makes it really clear what you're teaching in each particular topic, or what's being covered, if you're not doing the teaching.

If someone else is doing the teaching, someone you've hired, it still just keeps it really organized. It allows people to go to exactly the information that they want.

Another thing, when there's a collection of small problems, have lots of checklists and resources to make their jobs easier.

One thing I will tell you, and again, my latest newspaper column is based around this. People love collections of tools that do things for them, especially web links.

We're talking about creating info products.

You can find

a) you identify the problems that people have;

b) you identify either no or low-cost tools that they can access on the Internet, and you combine that with teaching them or explaining to them how to solve their problem.

Then explain how these little tools will help them solve each of these problems either faster, or with less effort, then you have a really winning combination.

You have something that people are going to get really, really, really excited about.

You also get into a situation where people say things like, "Wow! Just learning about that one thing, just learning about how to solve that one problem that's been bugging the hell out of me for all this time was worth the cost of the whole program."

That's when you know you have a winner. This makes it really, really easy.

Checklists and resources, and things like that, checklists are easy. You just rattle them off, or you find someone who knows and get them to rattle them off, pay them a few bucks, and go on your way.

As far as price points for products like this in the consumer market, you're really looking at $20 to $50, depending on the promise and the amount of information that you're doing.

If it's the top 10 problems-type thing, then you're probably going to get $10 or $20.

If it's 49 things that every web master needs to know, then you can probably knock it up to $39 or $49.

In a make-money type situation, then you can probably get up to about $97, somewhere along those lines.

What would I do if I had a niche market, where I had a collection of small problems? What would I do?

It's real simple.

"Your Own Profitable Info-Products In 72 Hours... (or Less!)"

I would line them up and knock them down. I would come up with a list of problems, and then just knock them out, explaining them as I went along.

One of the things you might immediately ask is, "Jim, what if there's a niche market I want to go after where I'm not the expert? What if I'm not the one who knows what to do, or I know some of it and I don't know all of it? What should I do? Does that mean I can't create a product?"

The answer to that is absolutely not!

Here's what I do, if there is or was something I didn't know the answer to. I'd do this. I'd do this in this order.

Number one, I'd bring in an expert to do an interview with. We'll talk about that more in a few minutes.

I would also then look for some public domain material.

I would look for something that was created by the US federal government. I would look for something that was created either in a magazine or in a book that had fallen into the public domain. We have lots of information about the public domain, again, in www.thenetreporter.com.

This isn't a course about public domain.

If you're interested in learning about the public domain and the mountains of content out there that you could use to create just about anything, and a lot of people do, then you need to learn about public domain material.

The next thing I would do, in this order.

First I'd try to interview an expert. Then I'd try to find some public domain material if I couldn't quickly get a hold of an expert.

If I couldn't find any public domain material, then I would hire somebody to research the answer to whatever the problem was.

Finally, what I would do would be to research the answer myself.

Why do I say this?

All of this, my researching the answer myself, is kind of like going back to college and being ignorant, and trying to figure everything out.

I'm not getting As, Bs, and Cs, based on my ability to figure something out. I'm a business owner trying to create information products.

If I can use somebody else's know-how or steal somebody else's know-how out of the public domain, it's not really stealing. But stealing is a great way to say it, or I can hire somebody to research the answer. I'm not getting paid with As, Bs, and Cs.

I'm getting paid with Ben Franklin, $100 bills. I don't want to be the one to do it if I can get somebody else to do it.

"Your Own Profitable Info-Products In 72 Hours... (or Less!)"

All I would do is just record everything, and turn it into an entry level product.

If I was doing an audio, I'd record it and turn it into a product. If I was doing it in screen capture video, then I would do that and turn it into a product.

I would not sit down and write it all out.

That would take forever, or relatively speaking, it would take forever, even though I'm a co-author of a book on *How to Write and Publish Your Own Ebook in as Little as 7 Days*.

I'm telling you right now.

That's probably the hardest way in the world to create anything other than the "book" that all of us have sitting in us.

I do believe all of us have at least one book sitting in us that needs to get out.

But once you get that book out, for the next one, there are some easier ways of doing it.

Blueprint #4 – Ongoing Problems

Blueprint number four, solving ongoing problems.

This is a niche where there is no end to the problem. There is no end. Once you've solved this problem, you've earned the right to solve some more and solve some more, and solve some more.

This isn't like selling your house. This isn't like getting your next mortgage. This isn't like learning how to type. This isn't like teaching your dog, potty training your dog.

This is stuff like how do I go and build my business, and take it to the next level every six months.

How do I maintain a wonderful, loving relationship with my spouse for the next 40 years as we grow and change, and our lives are different?

It's an ongoing issue. It's not based around an event. It's based around a lifestyle or who you are as a person, or your job.

As a real estate agent, how do I market and sell homes effectively in an ever-changing environment.

As new technology comes out and new competition, things are going to change. It's not going to stay the same.

The promise, when there's an ongoing problem, you want to get across to people that I'm the one, I'm the one who is going to do the thinking for you. I'm the one who's going to do the research, and keep you current to stay ahead of the problems.

I'm the one who will, most importantly, give you the information to stay ahead of your competition. I'm the one who will save you time, money, energy, and effort.

Think about it. For those of you who are members of www.thenetreporter.com, this what I do for you in the area of online business.

I do the thinking for you in a lot of respects. Not saying you can't think for yourself, but you have a lot of other stuff going on. You need a digest.

You need someone to stand out there and take a look at this, this, this, this, and this. See is this important? Is this significant? Is this something to pay attention to?

Also, I'm the one out there who's going to keep you current, and help you stay ahead of the problems, changes in pay-per-click strategies, changes in publishing methods, changes in multimedia and changes in all sorts of different areas.

I'm going to help you stay ahead of your competition. This saves you the time, energy, and effort of trying to figure it out on your own.

"Your Own Profitable Info-Products In 72 Hours... (or Less!)"

That's a great place to be, but you have to do that where there's a series of ongoing problems in that niche.

What product type should you come out with? What product types fit this model, this blueprint of ongoing problems?

The most obvious one is a membership site.

If there is a series of ongoing problems with no end in site, you should be looking at a membership site or a monthly newsletter. Some sort of an email newsletter would be the way I would look at it.

You can also look at some sort of physical continuity, whether that is some sort of a DVD of the month club or a physical newsletter. I would not recommend this one as an entry level, right out of the gate, physical continuity.

There are a whole lot of other variables that come into play that you don't want to deal with, especially for the 57% of you that don't have a product yet. Do not come out with a DVD of the month club or physical newsletter, as your first entry level product.

You're just asking for trouble.

Basically, what you're asking for, is not to get it done.

Another thing that I'm looking at would be something like a premium podcast, a subscription-based podcast. I think that's a neat idea, but it assumes that everybody who's going to buy from you has to have an iPod.

They have to not only have an iPod, but also the technical expertise to be able to subscribe to a podcast, and update their iPod on a regular basis to get the content from you. That really narrows the field.

Premium podcasting is getting a lot of play. But I think that it's still too specialized to look at real seriously, unless you have a pretty sophisticated and motivated online savvy audience.

As far as price points for doing some sort of continuity model in a consumer market, you're looking at between $17 and $47 a month, probably towards the lower end of that scale.

Think about it, and this is the way I look at it. Maybe this is wrong, but it's done me pretty well and stood me in good stead.

When I'm evaluating a consumer market, my first question is would my mom pay for that?

Does my mother, who is 69-years-old, female, living in America, have a basic understanding of the Internet, web surfing, things like that?

If my mom would buy it if she was in the niche, if she could buy it, meaning could she buy it mechanically and would she buy it, i.e. moneywise, then I think it's something good in a consumer market.

"Your Own Profitable Info-Products In 72 Hours... (or Less!)"

But if my mom wouldn't buy it and I couldn't see her buying it if she was a member of the niche market, then it gives me a cause to pause.

As far as make-money market, if you're looking to whack somebody monthly, you're probably looking somewhere in the $27 to $97 range.

I'll tell you right now. You have to work hard to get $97 a month from somebody. It takes a lot of work to get $97 a month out of somebody, even in a make-money market, when you're talking about individuals making that buying decision each month.

What would Jim do?

I would create a monthly membership site. The one thing I would really do is to systematize members expressing their ongoing problems on an ongoing basis.

I would take surveys often.

I would do most burning question pages. I would put those up. Anytime we were doing webinars or teleseminars, I would make ample opportunity for people to express problems and questions. That would provide the fodder for creating content for them, as we moved forward month after month after month.

If I wasn't the expert, I would use interviews to build the content. You can pay people with publicity and content. I would not pay people with money, if I could help it, to provide content for my membership site.

Paying with publicity is real easy.

You tell them, "Hey. Would you be interested in doing an interview on this and this topic? My members will be the ones who will receive the information, and then you can tell them about your book or about your site?"

I don't even need to use an affiliate link, if it's in a niche market or something like that, where it wouldn't really make any difference if you were using an affiliate link or not. They may not even have an affiliate link. They just want to push their book.

Another way you can pay them is with content.

"Hey. If you do this interview with me, I will give you a copy of the interview and it will be professionally packaged up. It will be well recorded, whatever, we have it transcribed. I'll give you the transcription. This is worth several hundred dollars that we're going to invest in this, hard cost, and I'll just give it to you. You can do whatever you want with it. It would be a nice bonus for your customers, whatever."

I would ***not*** pay somebody money, and I surely wouldn't give them a percentage of whatever I sold or with whatever was going on that month.

I would deliver it monthly, either in a webinar or teleseminar, or you could even do it as downloadable content.

Again, here's the pattern.

"Your Own Profitable Info-Products In 72 Hours... (or Less!)"

1. You record the content.
2. You have it transcribed, and
3. Then you use the transcription to create ebooks, special reports, articles, things in your archive.

Any time you interview anybody, any time you do monthly content, any time you have anything you do, drill this into your head. Always record it.

Always, eventually, get it transcribed.

Now you have it in different modalities that people can absorb, and it has a really high-perceived value.

Let's talk about the fastest products you can create to test a niche market...

The Fastest Products You Can Create - Interviews

The fastest products you can create, bar none, are audio products. Of the audio products, **the fastest audio product that you can create is an audio** *interview*.

Whether I had the expertise internally or not, if I needed to create a new product for a niche market, or an additional product for an existing niche that I was already in, I would do an interview. I do that all the time. I'm basically doing an interview now.

You just don't realize that I'm doing an interview, but I'm asking and answering questions without your even realizing it. You just interview yourself or an expert.

There are also a lot of sources of experts out there that you can find.

You can go to www.guru.com.

It's a great place if you did want to hire somebody, where you could find somebody.

Again, in www.thenetreporter.com we talk about this. We have a series of webinars we did on how to do interviews, where you can go to www.guru.com and just hire somebody for a couple of hours of their time.

"I would just like to hire you for a couple of hours, ask you some questions, and I have some students who are interested in this topic. It would be done as a work-for-hire. I will just interview you, and pay you whatever your typical hourly rate is. For a couple of hours, I want to talk to you about this topic."

Another place where you can find them, where I've known the owner of this site for years, is a place called "Radio-TV Interview Report."

It's at www.rtir.com.

There are experts there who want to be interviewed. If you told them, "Hey. I'd like to do an interview with you on this for my students. I'll give you a copy of the interview, and you can push your book or whatever."

That's another place where you can find people to do interviews.

You should also look, and it's not on here, at your own circle of influence. You should look at your own sphere of influence.

If you want to create a product in a niche, who do you know that knows something about that niche.

Let's say you were creating some type of quick-start guide or doing the thing where you were teaching them how to solve a bunch of little problems, or a bunch of problems that are just annoying.

"Your Own Profitable Info-Products In 72 Hours... (or Less!)"

Another thing that you need to realize about audio interviews is that you can use a combination of experts to create the product. Don't think that you have to get it all out of one person or one source.

I have that marked as top secret because people just don't think that way. They think, "Oh. I have to find an expert on this."

If you look at your topic and divide it up into three or four different areas, maybe you just need to find a couple, three experts, one on each of the areas.

Pay one, as far as www.guru.com, find another one from your sphere of influence, and find another one from the Internet or from somebody else, or a referral.

Compile it all into one product. It doesn't have to be just a mind suck on one person.

The other thing is, though, don't go to the extreme. Everybody says, "Oh, yeah. I could interview a bunch of Internet gurus about how to be an Internet guru."

Don't do that type of product. That's just annoying. Those don't sell anymore.

Another one is when you interview an expert and they have great information, but they suck as a presenter. Here's something that I've only seen a couple of people do, including myself.

What you do is rerecord the transcript with voice talent.

You can do, say a Mr. X-type interview.

You have somebody else read the answers and the whole spiel on it is like, "Look. We can't reveal who this person is because they don't want to cause friction in their industry. But we can tell you this person is this, this, this, and this."

You just give the credentials of the person that you interviewed.

"But we can't reveal who it is, because we don't want to have backlash or reprisals."

You just interview "somebody," and they just read the transcript so that they can liven it up and sound good.

You have an expert on a topic but they talk like this and they're about as entertaining and happy as someone who is one step away from jumping off a cliff.

Then you're going to have a situation where you might have great content, but the delivery sucks.

If you want to have an audio product, you need audio that's worth listening to.

This is something that you can do. Just take your transcript and have it reread by somebody who sounds excited and enthusiastic.

Another thing you can do is what I call a **"tips medley."**

"Your Own Profitable Info-Products In 72 Hours... (or Less!)"

That's another audio product that you can do. Just research a whole bunch of different issues or questions, or problems facing your audience, and address them all. Just really, in rapid fire fashion, do it in chunks.

You may have seen me do this in webinars before, where we play something called "beat the clock." Really all that is, is just a way of getting a whole bunch of information into a really short period of time.

I only give the person I'm interviewing three to four minutes to actually answer the question.

It keeps them focused. It keeps it really, really on point, in a 90-minute session. If you're only giving them 3 minutes to address something, a) they have to hit the point; and b) you're talking about 30 tips in a 90-minute period, somewhere between 20 and 30 tips.

A lot of times it's hard to get something out in 3 minutes, but in some cases they can give a really good tip in 1.5 minutes. You can average it out to about 20, 25, 30 tips in 90 minutes.

Another thing that you can do is flush this type of thing out with PDF schematics or mind maps, or links or resources.

You give the tips medley. You mention a bunch of different resources, and then they have, again, a cheat sheet, a checklist sheet, a resources sheet.

There they can get the notes taken for them, listen to it, get excited about it, have the sheet that they download and print off and that they use.

Another way to structure an audio product that works really well is similar to the tips medley. It's an **FAQ**, *frequently asked questions*. Just hit all their questions in rapid fire fashion.

Again, it's just a situation with an entry level product, where you want to cover as much ground as you can. That's a quick way of doing it.

What is "fast?"

What qualifies as fast for getting a good, unique info product ready to sell?

I'm curious. What do you think is fast? What would be fast enough for you? Let's qualify this though, what would be fast for you to have a good, unique info product ready to sell? Not, "How could I turn out some crap in an afternoon that nobody's going interested in?"

Here are the results of another (live) audience poll. I wanted to know what qualifies as *fast* when it comes to creating an original, unique info product?

- 24 hours start to finish.

- 48 hours start to finish.

- 72 hours start to finish.

"Your Own Profitable Info-Products In 72 Hours... (or Less!)"

- 1 week start to finish.

What I mean by that is not 24 hours total. If you were working 2 hours a day it would be 12 weeks or 12 days. But I mean you start at 8:00 this morning and by 8:00 tomorrow morning, you have something done.

What qualifies as fast to you?

Here are the results from our live audience.

- 7% - 24 hours start to finish.
- 9% - 48 hours start to finish.
- 32% - 72 hours start to finish.
- 52% - 1 week start to finish.

That actually surprises me. I figured everybody would check off 24 hours.

If you can get a product done in three, four, five days, and it was good and you could only put three or four hours a day into it, that would be pretty fast.

I'm going to show you exactly how to do that. First, I want to show you why I even thought that it was necessary to explain this.

"Your Own Profitable Info-Products In 72 Hours... (or Less!)"

Twitter Inspiration

I've done this before.

Actually, I've done this in about six hours, created a high-value, original, unique info product. But I'm weird. I'm strange. I've done this a bunch of times before.

Here's what made me think of this.

With one of my Platinum Mastermind members, Patty Rutkowski, I was following her on Twitter. Yeah, I'm on Twitter now. Am I posting all the time, like some sort of obsessive compulsive typing squirrel? No, but I do actually look at what people are doing.

I saw this, and Patty had written, "Write a book in a weekend…what? Like Nike says, just do it. I'll keep you posted."

I wasn't sure if Patty was thinking she wanted to write a book in a weekend, but I started thinking about it.

"Man! Write a book in a weekend? That would suck."

Doing it in a week is hard enough. But writing a real book in a weekend would suck if you sat down at page 1, blank, in Word, and were trying to figure it out.

I'm going to show you how you could actually write a book in a weekend, in just a minute. But by looking at this, I wanted to show you guys a really cool thing that I figured out. Maybe everybody knew it, but I started looking at it in a little bit different way.

Twitter's actually a fast way to find out questions that people are asking. It's virtually in real time on www.search.twitter.com.

If we go there, Twitter has a search function. It has all these different operators on it, kind of like with Google. You can put all these different search parameters and stuff.

You can search, let's do allergy relief, just to see who's talking about it, if anybody's talking about allergy relief.

You can look and see what people are talking about, any questions that they're asking, and things that they're talking about.

"If you have allergies, try something, something, allergy relief."

I was looking at this "write book," because of what Patty put in. I started looking at just the questions that people were asking, and it's all over the board.

But you can also put it in quotes to see who's talking about "write book."

"Get ready to teach how to write book in 30 days."

Please, why does it take 30 days, honey?

"Your Own Profitable Info-Products In 72 Hours... (or Less!)"

I was also looking on this at the questions, issues, things people are looking at. But then I saw something I'd never seen before. I saw something interesting.

There are a lot of other interesting things that this will do. In just a second, it should do something in here. After you sit here for a minute or two, if it's relatively active, it will come up and tell you that something else has come up.

There have been new things posted, that people have been asking about which to me shows that it's really, really hot.

Let's look at Swine Flu. Five seconds ago, somebody was talking about Swine Flu. In a few seconds, I guarantee up here, it's going to tell me that there have been new results for this actually posted.

Patty just said in the chat, "This is Patty. I really did write a book in a weekend called 'Job Search Party.'"

Good for you, Patty.

Right here it says, "Twenty-three more results since you started searching."

Does that mean Swine Flu is a hot topic? Absolutely it does!

I wanted to show you that this is a neat way, again, to look for questions that people are asking, a neat thing to see what people are concerned about. It's one way to start gathering intelligence about your particular niche audience.

You can see more of them have come in, as a result.

Step-By-Step What I'd Specifically Do, If I Only Had 48 to 72 Hours to Create a Unique Product

Let's talk about how you would create a product.

This is the fastest info product creation method that I know, for actually creating an original, high-value product in less than 72 hours, with the least amount of technical skill necessary.

I call this "The 72 Hour Product Formula."

"Your Own Profitable Info-Products In 72 Hours... (or Less!)"

Day 1 – Compile Questions

Step 1

Compile questions.

Let me take one step back and say, this is assuming that you have a niche audience, and you've identified a niche that you want to go after, preferably you've done a little bit of testing.

You know you can drive some traffic. You have a niche market that you're targeting, a group of people that you want to go after.

Step 1 is to **compile their top 25 questions or issues** that you want to address. You can find these questions from most burning question campaign.

If you have access to a list, or you have a list, you can run some ads, you can do a solo mailing, whatever.

You can buy a solo mailing, however, to drive people to a most burning question website that says, "Hey. What's your most burning question about _____?"

You can also do Google Group research.

Go to www.groups.google.com, do a search. Start searching the keywords, researching your niche audience, and see what questions they're asking.

You can do Twitter research like I just showed you. You can do forum research. Just take your main keyword phrase, and put in the keyword plus "forum."

"For sale by owner forum," would be a way you could find for sale by owner forums for people, who are looking to sell their house themselves.

Helpdesk research, if you have a helpdesk, for those of you when we did the survey talking about already having a product selling.

If you already have several products selling, you probably have a helpdesk or at least a help email where you can look back at the questions people ask repeatedly.

You can go and do some search engine research on Google.com. Do your keyword plus "frequently asked questions."

"For sale by owner frequently asked question."

"For sale by owner FAQ."

"Horse training FAQ."

"Horse training frequently asked questions."

Literally, search for those terms and you'll find where other people have assembled lists of questions.

"Your Own Profitable Info-Products In 72 Hours... (or Less!)"

You can also go to Google Answers, www.answers.google.com.

You can go to www.answers.yahoo.com, and search for questions that people are asking.

I'm *not* saying to steal their answer. You can't just go find somebody's FAQ page and have somebody read it off, record it, and call it your own. But nobody can copyright questions that people are asking (though they certainly ***can copyright their unique answers to the questions***).

Take those questions, and you come up with your list. Rephrase them, reposition them, and you're fine.

Step 1 is to compile the questions.

Ideally, you want to have at least 25 questions that you can ask. This is day 1. You're going to spend a few hours researching this, unless you can do a most burning question campaign.

I've done this before just with pay-per-click traffic, where we run an ad, start running an ad in the morning, and by the evening, we have 30, 40 questions that people have asked.

Does that happen every single time? No, that's actually, I would say, the exception to the rule. You have to do about ten most burning question campaigns to find the one that, right off the bat, is going to give you a whole bunch of questions right up front, without tweaking the page.

Step 1 is to compile your questions.

If you're motivated, in a four to six-hour period, you should be able to dig up 20, 25 questions.

Step 2, still on day 1, you want to get set to record.

You have two options.

Option one is to use a program like Sony Sound Forge, and a good microphone that you can get from my buddy, Mike Stewart at www.InternetAudioGuys.com.

That's if you're going to record the answers yourself, or if you're going to have live voice talent with you in your office or in your home, or you're going to go to them.

If I was going to interview my vet, then I would have an appointment with her. I'd carry my microphone and my laptop up to her office, and I'd sit there and pepper her with questions for an hour, hour and one-half. That would be one way to do it.

If you can't get access to the voice talent or if you don't want to buy a microphone or you just don't want to do that, then you have another option. I'm assuming you have a telephone.

Option two would be to use www.freeconference.com to record your audio as a conference call, and then you could download it as an MP3 file. You don't need any other equipment other than a phone.

www.freeconference.com, for $9 a month, they will give you unlimited recording capacity for a downloadable MP3.

"Your Own Profitable Info-Products In 72 Hours... (or Less!)"

That means even if you were the only one, you could set up a conference call, you could dial into the conference call.

You could interview yourself or have somebody else interview you, have a friend of yours, give them the list of questions.

They could ask you the questions, if you're the expert, or if you have an expert that you're going to interview, then you ask them the questions. They're on their end of the phone, and they answer the questions.

www.freeconference.com records it, and it's available to download within about two hours, minimum.

Some of you might say, "The phone quality sucks. Phones are not like studio."

If you want studio quality, then get a Sony Sound Forge and a real nice USB mic from Mike Stewart.

I just want to point out that right now, as of this recording, Microsoft is doing a million-dollar ad campaign, where the audio is nothing more than a phone conversation between an ad executive at Microsoft, and some big company executive that uses Microsoft products.

I've seen them do British Telecom, some place that make surfboards, and I forget who else.

The ad that they're spending millions of dollars to run is a telephone conversation with a bunch of weird graphics. I wouldn't worry about the audio quality so much, as much as getting the information out of people. You're sucking that information out of your expert, whether you're the expert or someone else is the expert.

That's day 1.

I'm not saying record it, because God forbid that you just knock it out really fast (wink).

I'm just saying compile all your questions, and then get set to record. You're either going to use Sony Sound Forge and a good microphone, or you're going to use www.freeconference.com.

Day 2 – Ask & Answer

With the 72-hour product formula day 2, what would you do the second day?

The second day, you're going to go through ask and answer. All that means is with whomever you're interviewing, whether it's you or somebody else, you're going to answer each question for about four to seven minutes each.

If they're open-ended questions that should be pretty easy to do, especially if whomever's being interviewed is truly an expert on the topic.

That means that 25 questions is going to yield somewhere between 100 and 175 minutes of audio content.

It depends on who's being interviewed, how much they elaborate, and how much you can elicit in additional information from them.

The bottom line, some questions are going to take a couple of minutes to answer, and other questions are going to take eight to ten minutes to answer. It's going to average out to somewhere around four or five minutes a pop. That's all you need.

Then what you do is take the audio and get it transcribed. The first place that I used for a couple of years was a place called www.idictate.com.

I haven't used them in awhile so their rates have probably changed, but the last time I used them, they charged $.0125 a word if you were the only one talking.

They charged $.02 a word if you were interviewing somebody.

I have transcriptionists that I use who actually charge less than that. Paying by the word is really the most expensive way of doing it typically, unless you speak really slowly.

A better way of buying transcription service is by the audio hour. But with www.idictate.com, as soon as you record it, you can upload it to iDictate, and you can get it done within about 24 hours. You don't have to have a relationship with them. You don't have to have anything other than a credit card. It's a fast way to get it done.

Typically, 100 to 175 minutes of audio content translates into somewhere around 45-plus pages of single spaced content. That's 12-point type. Again, that depends on how fast you or the person that you're interviewing talks.

That translates into about 90 pages of ebook content.

Then you put a header, a footer, you add graphics, you put not double space but space and one-half. You have a table of contents, index, all these other things.

Then you can stretch 45 pages of content up to about 90 pages, especially if you start adding some other things we're going to talk about in a second.

"Your Own Profitable Info-Products In 72 Hours... (or Less!)"

That audio also can turn into two to three physical CDs of content. An audio CD only holds around 70 minutes of content.

If you're up around 150-minute mark, you can put 50 minutes of content on each CD, and you have 3 physical CDs of content.

I would recommend this however, if you're thinking about doing a physical CD of your content rather than just offering in your product the MP3 download of the audio, as well as the transcript, the ebook version and the enhanced transcript version.

If you're going to do physical CDs that someone is going to play in their car, you really should do option one of recording it with a studio quality mic and Sound Forge. It's just going to sound a lot better.

It's going to be more like what people are expecting.

Not to say you can't have some phone-based content on an audio CD, but I will tell you that with audio CDs, people expect them to sound at a certain level.

Whereas with MP3, they're a lot more forgiving.

One thing I've learned that increases the value, you tell people MP3 so that you can play it on your iPod or other portable device.

For some reason, people think, "Oh, yeah. I can put that on my iPod and listen to it."

Day 3 – Add The Trimmings

The 72-hour product formula day 3, step 4, add the trimmings.

Once you have the bulk of your content done on day 2, then you can just add a 5-minute introduction. That's real easy.

Just tell people why it's important to learn this, and then give them an overview of what they're going to learn.

It might only end up being a couple, three minutes long, but you just make a little bulleted list of why it's important to learn this.

This is especially good for you if you're interviewing somebody else. It gives you a) something to say; and b) if you're looking to establish yourself personally in a niche, it puts you up on the same level as the expert or the experts that you're interviewing.

It really sets the tone for you as the presenter, and the person who's in charge. It's kind of like Larry King. Everybody knows who Larry King is. He's the guy who has the talk show on CNN.

If you think about it, who the hell is Larry King? He interviews other people and is on like his sixth wife.

But the fact that he's doing the intro, he's doing the conclusion, he's the one asking the questions and that makes him important.

You also want to add a five-minute conclusion. The conclusion is why what they learned is so great, and how it's going to impact their lives.

This is an old speaker's maxim.

Basically, tell them what you're going to tell them, and then tell them what you told them.

You do the exact same thing with an info product.

Tell them why they want to learn this and what they're going to learn, teach them, and then remind them why they wanted to learn it. Then tell why what they learned is so important, and how it's going to impact their lives in a whole bunch of different ways.

You also want to give them what to do next, give them homework, give them chapter assignments. That's another way to actually flush out your chunks, as well, especially if you're doing some sort of a how-to product.

Give them assignments at the end of the chapter.

"Based on what we just learned in this last module, this is what you should do. You should do this, this, this, and this, and here's a checklist for this."

"Your Own Profitable Info-Products In 72 Hours... (or Less!)"

Add things not just at the end, but also in between, because that will help dimensionalize it and add a lot of value.

Other things that you can add as trimmings, we've talked about **mind maps**. You can make all the free mind maps you want at a website called www.mindomo.com.

I've used it before. It's great. I use something now called www.mindjet.com, but that's $350.

www.mindomo.com will help you make really nice, basic mind maps that you can add.

You can give people lists of resources.

You can just use Word for that. Literally, just use Microsoft Word or some other word processor. Give them a list of resources, format it nicely, have headers and things like that, consistent texts and fonts, things like that.

A mind map is basically a spatial representation of things. It is a whole bunch of ideas arranged around a central idea.

A process map (often called a process map) is where you show somebody step-by-step how to go from point A to point Z. You've seen me do these before, as well.

I use a program called SmartDraw.

SmartDraw is not cheap either, but you can do a search for "free process mapping software" on Google. You will find pretty decent process mapping software that is just that. It's free.

Another way, though, that you can get people process maps is just to draw it out by hand and scan it in.

Sometimes, a hand-written document has a lot more impact than something that looks like it was created by a really expensive piece of software. I've used that to great effect, as well, because it really feels like they're getting behind-the-scenes information.

It's kind of like when I do whiteboard drawings on these webinars.

People feel, even though I can't really draw very well, they know to sit up and pay attention. This is the behind-the-scenes stuff. This isn't just some canned stuff. This is how I go from A to B to C to D. This is the actual process.

There's no problem putting those into your product, as well, to add value.

You can use Word, too. If you're good with your Microsoft Word or your word processor, you can create process maps just using arrows and text boxes to show people how to go from A to Z.

The big thing is just to convert everything to PDF.

If it's converted to PDF, then it's easily downloadable.

I've said this before about your first product, your fifth product, your tenth product. When you're just getting started but especially your first product, it should be downloadable.

"Your Own Profitable Info-Products In 72 Hours... (or Less!)"

It should be available from a minisite.

Make it easy on yourself. Let your website do the work. Let it build your list. Let it deliver the product. Let it take the money.

Let it do all of that independent of you, but you can't do it unless you're delivering everything as a downloadable product.

We've covered a lot here.

We've covered a ton, as far as product blueprints, how to create a product really, really quickly, what I would do in specific situations, four specific product blueprints based on the specific problems, levels of problems, amount of problems and ongoing problems of your particular niche audience.

This was a lot for you to absorb.

I have a quick question for you (live audience). For our last poll of the evening, how likely are you to use what you've learned tonight and apply it to your business?

Your choices are:

- Very likely, I'm ready to take things to the next level now.

- Likely, I'm going to take action within the next week.

- Unlikely, I'm not sure this will work for me.

- Very unlikely, this stuff doesn't work.

This is kind of my report card. This is your feedback.

Let's take a look at the results.

- 56% - Very likely, I'm ready to take things to the next level now.

- 41% - Likely, I'm going to take action within the next week.

- 3% - Unlikely, I'm not sure this will work for me.

For the 3%, *The Net Reporter* may not be right for you. I'll just tell you that right now. This is the kind of stuff that we teach. This is all about info products and information publishing.

I know that's going to sound kind of harsh, but after what we just went through, I'm not sure this is going to work for you.

All I can tell you is that maybe this isn't for you or you don't have a niche market that you know enough about, in order to know that this could be applied.

I would encourage you, if that's the case, to really review the information we have in *The Net Reporter* about how to research niche markets, how to get a handle on what they're looking for.

"Your Own Profitable Info-Products In 72 Hours... (or Less!)"

For the 97% of you who are going to take action on this, please do. I have some final thoughts for you to kind of keep it all in perspective, what you should do next.

Final Thoughts

Again, keep this really, really simple.

I think you know what's about to happen, what I'm about to tell you. It's actually really, really simple what you should do next.

You should take action.

If you don't have an info product, you need to use what you've just learned to make one.

Let's say it took you a couple of days to research the questions.

Let's say it took you a day to get ready to do the recording. That means signing up for www.freeconference.com and paying the $9, even though that should only take about 15 minutes.

Let's say that took a whole day, and then let's say you took a day to find your expert or even two days or even three days to find an expert.

That still gives you the seventh day to get them on the phone, and do the recording, which is going to be the bulk of your product.

Just do something. Do it.

If you don't have an info product, you've learned to make one. There are no excuses.

If you have an info product, then what you need to do is use what you've learned to make another one.

Use what you've learned to kind of reposition your thinking about what do people want, what level of problem do they have?

What type of problem do they have, and what's the best way to position the offer to help them.

Then, if I don't have the expertise, how can I go find someone who does have the expertise to create the content that I can sell them, either up front, in an entry level product, or as a membership site?

The bottom line is, just keep it simple, price it right, and get it done. That's a great mantra, by the way, for anybody who sells information on the Internet.

Keep it simple.

Price it right.

Get it done.

I'm Jim Edwards. Have a great day, and we'll talk to you soon.

Bulk Book Order & Customized Version Information

Most **AQuickReadBook.com** titles are available at special quantity discounts for bulk purchases for sales promotions, premiums, fundraising, gifts or educational use.

In other words, if you'd like to get a truckload of copies of this book (or even just a dozen or two) to hand out at an event, company function, or as gifts to your clients, we can help you out at a substantial discount over the cover price.

Just contact us and we'll get you a quote. ☺

Also, special customized / company specific versions or excerpts can be created to fit specific needs. So if you'd like to do something customized with this book, drop us a line and we'll discuss it with you.

Our goal is to help you get what you need and to help our authors help as many people as possible with their books.

For more information, please contact us at A Quick Read Book™ online at www.AQuickReadBook.com

## More Help From Jim Edwards

Find out more about Jim's latest projects here:

Jim's SPECIAL OFFER

The Net Reporter
"Fast Track Video Coaching"

You get access to Jim's 6-Module "Fast Track Video Coaching" sessions that will take you Step-By-Step from ZERO to your own crazy profitable online business faster than you ever dreamed possible- a $997 Value - FREE!

* Module 1: Mindset & Niche Market Research
* Module 2: Getting your Web Presence up fast
* Module 3: Your Sales Message
* Module 4: Your Own High-Value Product
* Module 5: Fast Targeted Traffic
* Module 6: List Building

Get all the details here:

www.TheNetReporter.com/ftvc

"Your Own Profitable Info-Products In 72 Hours... (or Less!)"

NOTES:

"Your Own Profitable Info-Products In 72 Hours... (or Less!)"

NOTES:

The IMBIBLE

The Imbible

A Cocktail Guide
for Beginning & Home Bartenders

Micah LeMon

University *of* Virginia Press
Charlottesville & London

University of Virginia Press • © 2017 by the
Rector and Visitors of the University of
Virginia • All rights reserved • Printed
in Canada on acid-free paper
First published 2017
9 8 7 6 5 4 3 2 1
Photography by Tom McGovern

Page 8: A Midnight Modern Conversation, William Hogarth, 1732. (Wellcome Library, London)

Library of Congress Cataloging-in-Publication Data • Names: LeMon, Micah, 1979– author.
Title: The imbible : a cocktail guide for beginning and home bartenders / Micah LeMon.
Description: Charlottesville : University of Virginia Press, 2017. | Includes bibliographical
references and index. Identifiers: LCCN 2017018767| ISBN 9780813940380 (cloth : alk.
paper) | ISBN 9780813940434 (e-book) Subjects: LCSH: Cocktails. |
Bartending—Handbooks, manuals, etc. | LCGFT: Cookbooks.
Classification: LCC TX951 .L45 2017 | DDC 641.87/4—dc23
LC record available at https://lccn.loc.gov/2017018767

Contents

Introduction • 2

1. Theory • 5
2. Tools & Techniques • 51
3. Stirred & Shaken Cocktails • 79
4. Making Your Own Signature Cocktails • 173

Appendix 1:
Bitters, Cordials & Other Preparations • 181

Appendix 2:
Commonly Used Terms behind the Bar • 197

Notes • 201

Recommended Reading • 205

Index • 207

The IMBIBLE

Introduction

I started bartending before I'd ever had a drink. The first time I stepped behind a bar, I had absolutely no idea what I was doing. I knew a grand total of nothing about alcohol. I didn't drink, and my parents didn't either. And coming from an Evangelical *and* Pentecostal Christian background, there was a certain amount of fear, trembling, and exhilaration I experienced my first couple times pouring drinks. I thought God might strike me dead with lightning, give me leprosy, or inflict some equally biblical punishment just for touching the stuff. But after the shock of being around a bar full of sinful booze washed over me, I was immediately curious. What was in all these bottles? What the hell is vermouth? And more importantly, how do you make all this firewater taste even remotely palatable? Do drinkers have warped palates? Is it possible to make a delicious cocktail, and if so, how?

In those first days bartending, I wish someone had handed me this book. In the lazy days behind the Sunday brunch bar, I combed Mr. Boston's bar book and every other dusty recipe book I could get my hands on. They were long on recipes and short on insight. What makes a balanced drink? What techniques did I need to master? How could I make an original "Micah" (!) cocktail? Thumbing through the books shift after shift never yielded insights or answers.

Fortunately, in the past decade or so there's been a renewed interest in transforming raw and aggressively alcoholic ingredients into balanced and delicious cocktails. But in examining the pantheon of current and historical cocktail books, I still found one glaring gap on the shelf: a book that takes home and new bartenders on an efficient tour of theory, technique, and tools, so that they can properly execute classic cocktails and have the insight to riff on those to create cocktails of their own. I hope to fill that gap with this book.

To start, I'll be introducing basic cocktail theory. We'll look at what components are needed to make a balanced cocktail, and we'll examine each of those basic components in detail. Then we'll discuss the techniques and tools necessary to get you behind the bar quickly. Next, we'll look at two classes of cocktails—stirred and shaken—and examine an archetype in each class. In that chapter we'll be exploring my thesis: all original cocktails are theoretically sound riffs on existing, classic cocktails. Knowledge of the classics, along with basic theoretical knowledge, informs and structures all successful attempts to make original drinks. Finally, I'll present some simple tables that show the endless possibilities for creating new drinks when you're equipped with a successful starting point and a basic understanding of cocktail theory.

I
Theory

As I mentioned, I started bartending long before I'd ever had a drink. I got a job at a country club while I was in college, and one night they were short a banquet bartender. Being a straight-A student, and being totally unfamiliar with alcohol, I saw bartending as a fun elective (I had only one fun elective in four years of college). I remember my first time behind the bar opening the handles of Dewar's, Bacardi, and Absolut, giving them a sniff, and thinking "Yuck!" These spirits seemed so potent to my virgin nostrils! They were even more aggressive on my palate. From the very first moments of learning to bartend, I had a secret: I thought booze tasted disgusting.

In fact there is some research that suggests that lab animals unfamiliar with the post-ingestive effects of highly alcoholic drinks will actively choose to *avoid* imbibing them. I felt a bit like one of those animals the first summer I worked at the club. I made super-boozy Old Fashioneds (yuck!) and vermouthless Martinis (even worse!), and generally I recoiled any time I tasted the drinks I made for members. What kept me doing it was: 1) it was a decent job for a nineteen-year-old, and 2) it opened up a whole other world where people who would never speak to me under normal circumstances would become friendly, even chatty, and would actively solicit my opinions. And for me, just a little von Hövel riesling made me feel like a king. The real challenge was this: how could I ever make rich, balanced, and delicious cocktails with spirits that were themselves so strong, aggressive, and unpalatable?

Historical Approaches to Making Balanced Cocktails

The answer is simple: a sound theoretical approach. Let's back up just a few hundred years and look at some historical approaches to taming the flame of humankind's firewater, and why they matter to our discussion.

PUNCH

Perhaps the most elaborate and successful method of mellowing spirits originated in India around the seventeenth century. The Hindis of southern India at the time had plenty of sugarcane, and some evidence suggests that they were not only making sugar wine as early as the time of Christ, they were also distilling it into rum (sometimes referred to as "arak" or "arrack"). To tame the flavor of this raw spirit, they added tea, a sugar syrup infused with citrus peels, and other spices, nutmeg being the most common. From a culinary perspective,

this drink makes a great deal of sense: the spirit provides an alcohol backbone for the drink, the sugar syrup sweetens the booze, the acidity of the citrus and tannins of the tea balance the sweetened booze mixture, and the spice provides an additional dash of complexity. *Panch* actually means "five" in Hindi, referring to the five ingredients present in a successfully balanced panch: spirit, sugar, citrus, spice, and water. When British sailors discovered this pleasant and sophisticated beverage, they fell in love with it. They brought the tradition of "punch" back home, and punch houses became all the rage in England in the seventeenth and eighteenth centuries.

THE "COCK-TAIL"

While drinksmiths were elaborately concocting punch in England, the state of drink making in the American colonies in the 1700s was decidedly more spartan. Tea and citrus were luxury items for many colonists, and the most common way of trying to tame the bite of the grain distillates of the day was to add sugar and just a bit of water. They called this spirit-sugar-water concoction a *sling*. Like many

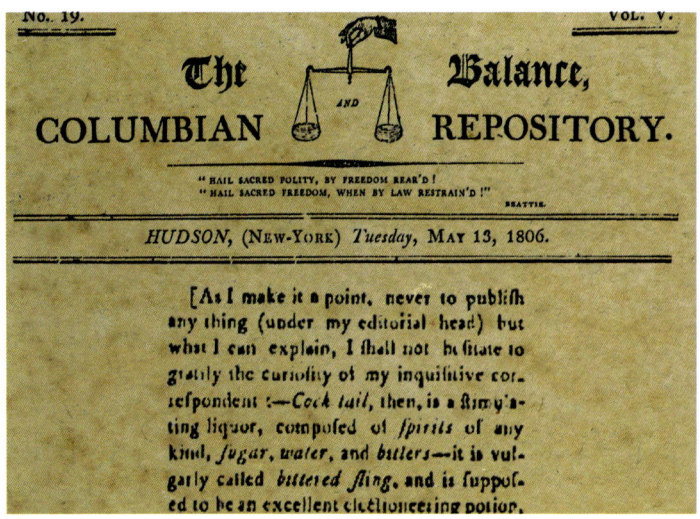

societies, the American colonies struggled to responsibly incorporate distillates into their daily lives without over-imbibing, and drunkenness and hangovers were a daily problem. "Hair of the dog" was the most common prescription for having over-imbibed the night before, and health-conscious colonists would likely add just a bit of medicine to their morning sling in the form of medicinal bitters. What they did not expect, however, was that the bitter note from the medicine did wonders to balance the sugared booze in the drink. Through attempting to mitigate a hangover, the American "cock-tail" was born. In 1806, the word *cock-tail* appeared in print, and America, believe it or not, was teetering on becoming the best place in the world to get a drink.

THE ICE TRADE

Prior to the 1800s, most beverages were served hot or lukewarm. The most common way of heating a beverage à la minute in a tavern was, strangely enough, plunging a red-hot iron into the drink. Dave Arnold, beverage director at the French Culinary Institute, is the only guy to date to do any research on hot pokers, and a good deal of his data indicates that this approach to drink making doesn't jibe well with the modern palate.

Then in the early 1800s, drinking habits started to change. About the same time the word *cock-tail* first appeared in print, a New England entrepreneur named Frederic Tudor had a great idea: cut ice out of frozen lakes in the winter and store blocks of it in insulated warehouses for sale in the summer. By 1833, Tudor's company was shipping New England ice as far away as Calcutta, India—all before most city residents on any continent had potable water or refrigerators. The blossoming ice trade had a dramatic effect on American drinking culture in the years that followed, and American bartenders soon invented a new set of tools and techniques to process ice and mix iced drinks.

this drink makes a great deal of sense: the spirit provides an alcohol backbone for the drink, the sugar syrup sweetens the booze, the acidity of the citrus and tannins of the tea balance the sweetened booze mixture, and the spice provides an additional dash of complexity. *Panch* actually means "five" in Hindi, referring to the five ingredients present in a successfully balanced panch: spirit, sugar, citrus, spice, and water. When British sailors discovered this pleasant and sophisticated beverage, they fell in love with it. They brought the tradition of "punch" back home, and punch houses became all the rage in England in the seventeenth and eighteenth centuries.

THE "COCK-TAIL"

While drinksmiths were elaborately concocting punch in England, the state of drink making in the American colonies in the 1700s was decidedly more spartan. Tea and citrus were luxury items for many colonists, and the most common way of trying to tame the bite of the grain distillates of the day was to add sugar and just a bit of water. They called this spirit-sugar-water concoction a *sling*. Like many

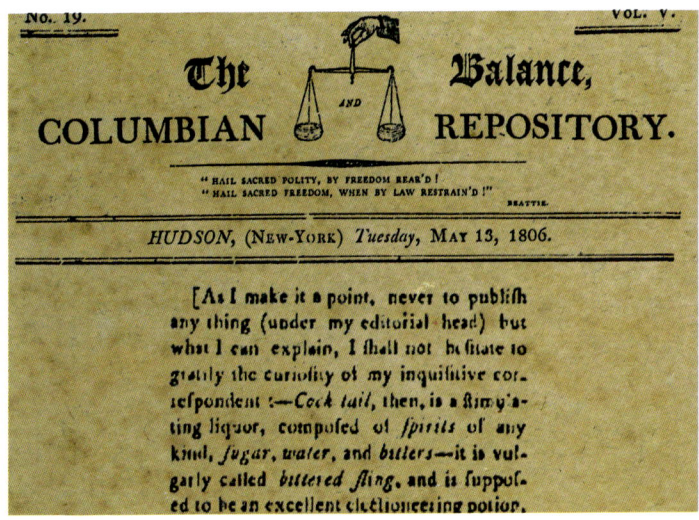

societies, the American colonies struggled to responsibly incorporate distillates into their daily lives without over-imbibing, and drunkenness and hangovers were a daily problem. "Hair of the dog" was the most common prescription for having over-imbibed the night before, and health-conscious colonists would likely add just a bit of medicine to their morning sling in the form of medicinal bitters. What they did not expect, however, was that the bitter note from the medicine did wonders to balance the sugared booze in the drink. Through attempting to mitigate a hangover, the American "cock-tail" was born. In 1806, the word *cock-tail* appeared in print, and America, believe it or not, was teetering on becoming the best place in the world to get a drink.

THE ICE TRADE

Prior to the 1800s, most beverages were served hot or lukewarm. The most common way of heating a beverage à la minute in a tavern was, strangely enough, plunging a red-hot iron into the drink. Dave Arnold, beverage director at the French Culinary Institute, is the only guy to date to do any research on hot pokers, and a good deal of his data indicates that this approach to drink making doesn't jibe well with the modern palate.

Then in the early 1800s, drinking habits started to change. About the same time the word *cock-tail* first appeared in print, a New England entrepreneur named Frederic Tudor had a great idea: cut ice out of frozen lakes in the winter and store blocks of it in insulated warehouses for sale in the summer. By 1833, Tudor's company was shipping New England ice as far away as Calcutta, India—all before most city residents on any continent had potable water or refrigerators. The blossoming ice trade had a dramatic effect on American drinking culture in the years that followed, and American bartenders soon invented a new set of tools and techniques to process ice and mix iced drinks.

The Necessary Components of a Balanced Cocktail

By the mid-nineteenth century, America became known not only for its ice, but also for its iced cocktails. "The Professor" Jerry Thomas was one of many "mixologists" who ushered in a golden age of cocktails in the United States. Their approach to making drinks paid homage to both punch and the "cock-tail": they started with a base spirit, sweetened that spirit with sugar, and balanced the boozy-sweet mixture with something assertively acidic (à la punch) or bitter (à la the cock-tail). By the end of the century the techniques, recipes, tools, and general approaches to making drinks were set and codified for the trade of bartending. Thomas and his cohort's strategy survives today and forms the theoretical basis for creating a balanced cocktail: *start with a spirit, sweeten it, balance it with something assertively acidic or assertively bitter.*

Three components are needed for a balanced cocktail:

SPIRIT • SWEET • SOUR/BITTER

The *spirit* is there to provide the alcohol backbone of a drink; the *sweet* is there to mask the overwhelming booziness of the spirit; and a *sour/bitter* component is there to balance the sweetened booze. (A much less common but still valid way to balance sweetened booze is by using something fatty or savory to tie together the spirit and sweet components; see the Kentucky Alexander recipe in chapter 3 for an example.)

When I look at a recipe, I try to understand how the ingredients listed fit into what is required for a balanced beverage. Similarly when constructing a recipe, I want to have all of the requisite components present to give myself an optimal chance at making a balanced and tasty beverage. One of the more illuminating exercises for me has been reviewing and examining classic recipes. Classic cocktails are blueprints for successful drinks, and mastering a classic recipe can serve as a roadmap to a new creation or (as often happens) to recreating a successful drink that already exists.

Let's take a look at a classic cocktail, classify the components, and think about how we might substitute one like ingredient for another like ingredient to make a new drink. Consider a classic Daiquiri:

> 2 OZ. RUM
>
> ½ OZ. SIMPLE SYRUP
>
> ½ OZ. FRESH LIME JUICE

How do these ingredients fit into the three components we need for a balanced cocktail? Let's look at that:

Rum	Spirit
Simple syrup	Sweet
Lime juice	Sour

What if we substituted a different spirit for rum? How about tequila? That would give us:

Rum → tequila	Spirit
Simple syrup	Sweet
Lime juice	Sour

And what if we substituted an orange liqueur, a sweet component, for the existing sweet component in the recipe? We'd have the following:

Tequila	Spirit
Simple syrup → orange liqueur	Sweet
Lime juice	Sour

Look familiar? It's a Margarita! This method of substituting like ingredient for like ingredient is called the Mr. Potato Head approach to bartending, and it is by no means my intellectual property. Rather, it is a common human strategy of classifying things, substituting like for like, and then seeing what hilarity or serendipity ensues. All bartenders, most chefs, and most creative people, whether they realize it or not, use the Mr. Potato Head method when riffing on existing cocktails, dishes, and ideas, respectively. If you recognize that something is an ear or nose or pair of eyes, then you intuitively know where and how to plug it into an existing scaffold that all makes sense to your brain. It's the same with drinks: start with a successful scaffold, classify your ingredients, and substitute like ingredient for like ingredient. It's an alarmingly simple idea that really helps to demystify all the arcane bottles, mysterious ingredients, and grandiosely peacocking bartenders.

This method is something that we'll be exploring in depth in the recipes in chapter 3. My thesis is that nearly all successful cocktails can be reduced to a stirred or shaken archetype. Making new, creative drinks is really a matter of mastering those archetypes, classifying the ingredients into the requisite categories, and using the Mr. Potato Head approach to substitute like ingredient for like ingredient.

"IT NEED TO BE YUMMY"

A significant challenge in making cocktails comes after learning to balance your requisite ingredients. I currently work with an opinionated French chef. As a part of staying on top of his craft, he frequently travels to New York, San Sebastian, Paris, and other big food cities to see what other chefs are doing. Much of the time when he comes back he is either annoyed or underwhelmed. When I press him for more specific criticism, he nearly always says the same thing in his thick French accent: "Food . . . it need to be tasty; it need to be yummy." He laments having paid 150 euros to eat moss plated on dirt, cow tendon, and cod tongue, and pines instead for a perfectly braised lamb shank with a smart and well-executed sauce and starch. That is to say, even when a dish is visionary, innovative, and even balanced, the response should always be, "Yummy!"

What is *yummy*? Admittedly, it's something that's hard to define. Sometimes it's immediate and reflexive, and sometimes it evolves as a stimulus passes over your palate. It involves not only understanding balance and using proper technique but also pairing flavors that get along.

So how do you make drinks that are not only balanced and technically sound, but also yummy? The answer is, not surprisingly, common sense. Knowledge of classic cocktails, as I've mentioned before, is a good place to start, as these drinks not only serve as blueprints for your own creative riffs, they also provide historically successful flavor pairings. There are also plenty of resources that can help you spitball some potentially successful pairings. The recommended reading section in the back of this book is a good place to start. And finally, use your palate! Do you like your drink? Is it yummy? Is it balanced but the flavors are muddled? Do you need to bring balance to it, or do you need to rethink your ingredients?

In the following pages, I elaborate on our necessary theoretical components: spirit, sweet, and sour/bitter. First we'll cover spirits, how they are produced, how they differ from one another, some of my preferred pairings, and some of my preferred brands. Next we'll talk sweets, and I'll give you some basic pointers on making fun syrups of your own. Finally we'll talk sour/bitter, spending a decent amount of time talking about all the strange, bitter ingredients popular in centuries past that survive only in cocktails.

Spirits

When we say *spirits,* we're talking about distillates. Distillation is a simple process in which two or more liquids are separated by heating the mixture until the more volatile component evaporates, then collecting that vapor and condensing it back into a liquid. Distillers distill wines (fruit ferments) and beers (grain ferments) to get the "spirit" of the original ferment. In a vat of fermented grape juice (wine), there are a host of other molecules (esters, aldehydes, methanol, acetone, fusel oils, acetaldehyde) in addition to just water and alcohol. A distiller's job is to select or exclude those auxiliary elements in a way that best represents the "spirit" of the wine. That spirit can be aged, flavored, or redistilled to progressively scrub the spirit of any molecules other than ethanol (ethyl alcohol, or simply alcohol) and a trace of water. When that happens, we say the spirit is *neutral.* Most spirits, both neutral and nonneutral, have a measure of water added just prior to bottling to bring them down to bottling proof, around 40 percent alcohol by volume (ABV) or 80 proof. One of the more helpful ways to think about spirits for me has been to classify them not by what they are made from but rather by how much of the flavor of the original wine or beer shows up in the final spirit. Vodka and gin are most frequently made with a neutral base, so let's talk about them first.

VODKA

Production: Vodka can be made from any fermentable starch source. It is distilled until neutrally flavored, and then filtered through charcoal to remove any residual base flavor.

Flavor notes: Vodka generally has a pure ethanol smell, and vanishes quickly in the presence of other flavors. It's a good candidate for mixing when you have a very delicate flavor you don't want to overwhelm, and when you want the spirit to provide structure for the drink without too much flavor.

Pairings: Vodka is classically paired with savory things (e.g., Bloody Marys, dirty Martinis with olive brine) but is also great with delicate flavors like melon, tea, herbs, white vermouth, and citrus.

Other notes: Vodka came into popularity after the golden age of American cocktails (c. 1835–1920), which means that it is not represented in the pantheon of golden age cocktails. Modern bartenders have tended to pooh-pooh vodka because of its lack of flavor, but in the right context, it's the bottle you want to reach for.

Micah's picks: As this stuff is distilled neutral, it's not worth spending a fortune on a bottle. I frequently reach for Stolichnaya and Reyka, and in a pinch even Smirnoff will do.

GIN

PRODUCTION: Gin is usually made with a neutral base and flavored with botanicals, juniper being the most conspicuous in most gins. In fact, the word *gin* comes from *juniper*.

PAIRINGS: As there is considerable variability in styles of gin (see below), there are similarly a myriad of pairings. But generally speaking, gin shows up where vodka would vanish, and the juniper and botanicals come through in the resulting cocktail. Gin adds a botanical complexity, and a few of my go-to pairings with gin overlap vodka: green herbs, melons, tea, white vermouth, bittersweet cordials, stone fruit, and citrus.

OTHER NOTES: Not all gins fit the juniper-heavy style, so it's worth parsing gin into some subcategories so we can Mr.-Potato-Head a little more effectively.

> **LONDON DRY:** Classic, juniper-heavy gin with no sugar added. Made from a neutral base and not aged.
> **MICAH'S PICKS:** Tanqueray gins, Hayman's Navy Strength, Beefeater, Greenall's, Bombay gins.

OLD TOM: Old Tom indicates that the gin may be either aged (until it takes on a brown hue) or sweetened slightly, or both. It may also have a nonneutral, grain-forward spirit base. Old Tom was a popular style in the mid- to late nineteenth century and appears in some classic cocktail recipes. **MICAH'S PICKS:** Hayman's Old Tom, Ransom Old Tom, Bluecoat Barrel Finished, Barr Hill Reserve Tom Cat.

PLYMOUTH: Plymouth brand gin is the only surviving example of the Plymouth style, which stands in contrast to the London dry style by being a little lighter on the juniper and more earthy and peppery. **MICAH'S PICKS** *(the only picks!):* Plymouth, Plymouth Navy Strength.

NEW AMERICAN/OTHER: Many American and contemporary gins are attempts to redefine gin. These gins can be made with neutral spirits or not, aged or unaged, and can be light or heavy on the juniper. **MICAH'S PICKS:** Uncle Val's Botanical (heavy lemon, tangerine, citrus notes), Barr Hill (heavy juniper notes and finished with a touch of honey), Hendrick's (cucumber and flowery notes), Ransom Dry (assertive grain base with heavy spice and juniper).

NONNEUTRAL SPIRITS ARE distillates that taste like the wine or beer they are made from. The assertive flavors of these clear distillates can be softened or "solved" by aging with wood. The ethanol in the distillates interacts with several organic compounds in the wood resulting in a softened and richer mouth feel, and many aged spirits bear these signature, wooden-barrel flavors: vanilla, oak, toasted wood, dried fruit, caramel, honey, and toffee.

RUM

PRODUCTION: Rum is made from sugarcane and sugarcane byproducts. Most rum is made cheaply with molasses, a starch-rich byproduct of processing raw sugarcane into table sugar. Other varieties such as rhum agricole and cachaça are distilled directly from fermented sugarcane juice. All varieties of rum can be aged or unaged.

FLAVOR NOTES: Rum distillers frequently try to retain the molasses's marshmallow and licorice richness and complexity in the final spirit. Sugarcane distillates like rhum agricole and cachaça are frequently more raw on the palate than molasses distillates.

PAIRINGS: The classic pairing with rum is fruit, fruit, and more fruit. I tend to agree; I like to pair rum with tropical fruit and citrus, especially lime. Other pairings include cream, coffee, baking spices, tea, rich sherries, herbs, vermouths, and bittersweet cordials that echo rum's common vanilla and nutty notes.

OTHER NOTES: Rum was the main player in the tiki cocktail movement of the 1930s through the 1960s. One of the main contributions of this movement was repopularizing the approach of splitting the spirit portion of a drink into several different types of spirits, in this case a blend of different styles of rum. The blended spirit base created flavor complexity that would have been lacking had a single distillate been used.

MICAH'S PICKS: Aged rums: Pusser's rums, Appleton's aged rums, Mount Gay Rums, Zaya, Depaz rhum agricole, Smith and Cross. Unaged rums: Vitae Platinum, Wray & Nephew Overproof, Leblon cachaça, Bacardi Silver.

Zaya
APPLETON ESTATE
RARE BLEND
12
1749
SMITH & CROSS
LONDON
TRADITIONAL JAMAICA RUM
PUSSER'S RUM
DEPAZ
APPLETON ESTATE
SIGNATURE BLEND
MOUNT GAY
1703
Barbados Rum

WRAY & NEPHEW
White
OVERPROOF RUM
PRODUCT OF JAMAICA
J. WRAY & NEPHEW LTD
BACARDÍ
SUPERIOR
RON SUPERIOR CARTA BLANCA
ESTABLECIDO EN 1862
SANTIAGO DE CUBA
LEBLON
CACHAÇA
VITAE
SPIRITS
PLATINUM RUM

MEZCAL

Production: Mezcal is a distillate made in Central America from several different species of agave plants. The agaves used to make mezcal need to be heated to break down the complex carbohydrates in the plant into fermentable sugars. The most traditional way to do this is to cook the piñas, or sugar-rich agave hearts, in an earthen oven with hot stones and embers. Mezcals may be aged or unaged.

Flavor notes: Cooking the piñas this way imparts unmistakable smoky and earthy notes that show up prominently in the final distillate. Tequila is a specific type of mezcal produced from only one species of agave in a geographically limited area of Mexico. Piñas used to make tequila are usually cooked in ovens as opposed to in earthen pits, and the resulting distillate lacks the smoke and earth of other mezcals and instead features the agave flavors more prominently.

Pairings: Mezcal's smokiness makes it cut through whatever you throw at it. I like to pair it with big flavors: habanero and other

spicy or smoky peppers, and acidic flavors like passion fruit, marmalade, and pineapple. The smoky notes also make swapping in mezcal in place of a smoky scotch not an altogether outrageous idea. I like to pair tequila with flavors that echo agave: melons, cucumbers, pineapple, white vermouth, and citrus. Beet, prickly pear, turmeric, and other earthy or rooty flavors are also fun with tequila and mezcal.

OTHER NOTES: Mezcal and tequila, like vodka, were not popular in the American cocktail golden age, and are conspicuously absent from lists of famous pre-Prohibition cocktails. When buying tequila, be certain the label reads "100 percent agave." Many tequilas are cut with neutral spirits to fill more bottles, and this cut comes with a loss of flavor and quality.

MICAH'S PICKS: Don Julio tequilas, Herradura tequilas, Tequila Ocho tequilas, Del Maguey mezcals, Los Amantes mezcals.

WHISK(E)Y

Whisk(e)y is most commonly made from corn, rye, wheat, or barley. Whiskies are generally classified by what grain is used to make the distillate, and most geographic areas have preferred grains and methods of production. In many cases a blend of grains is used, and that grain blend or "mash bill" can have a big effect on the final product.

A quick note on when to use the *e:* Generally speaking, Scottish, Canadian, and Japanese distillers choose to call their whiskies *whisky* while American distillers use *whiskey,* although there are some exceptions—Maker's Mark Bourbon Whisky, in particular. Opening the bottle and having a sip will tell you more about the whisk(e)y than an "e" will. It will also be a little more fun!

In that spirit, let's look at the production, flavor notes, and pairings of our most common whiskies.

RYE WHISKEY

PRODUCTION: Rye whiskey is a grain distillate made of at least 51 percent rye. To be called rye whiskey in the United States, this distillate must also be aged in charred new oak containers.

FLAVOR NOTES: Think rye bread, caraway seed, and a hint of clove. Rye has an unmistakable breadiness and spiciness that makes it ideal for certain applications.

PAIRINGS: Rye is famous for getting along with sweet vermouth, and is generally a historical go-to in stirred cocktails featuring bitters and bittersweet cordials. I also like pairing rye with birch, sassafras, orange, lemon, pineapple, mint, and pumpkin.

OTHER NOTES: Rye can be light, spicy, and bready, or richer and much more mellow, becoming almost bourbon-like. Rye can have a high percentage of corn (the primary grain in bourbon) in the mash bill, and conversely bourbon can have a high percentage of rye, making some bourbons and ryes overlap just a bit on the palate.

Micah's picks: Old Overholt, Rittenhouse, Wild Turkey ryes, Pikesville 110, Bulleit Rye.

BOURBON WHISKEY

Production: Bourbon is a grain distillate made of at least 51 percent corn and usually fermented with some combination of rye, wheat, or barley. To be called bourbon in the U.S., this distillate also must be aged in charred new oak containers. Notice that a whisk(e)y *does not* have to be made in Bourbon County, Kentucky, to be called bourbon in the U.S.

Flavor notes: With bourbon especially, the mash bill can dramatically affect the final distillate. Lots of rye in the bill makes the bourbon more spicy, lots of barley makes it more scotch-like, and lots of wheat allows more corn sweetness to come through. When I think of bourbon, I think of the soft caramel corn flavor that makes it perfect for certain pairings.

PAIRINGS: I like to use bourbon with stone fruit, bittersweet cordials, bitters, brown sugar, caramel, cream, orange, rich sherries, and winter citrus (kumquat, grapefruit, and Meyer lemon especially).

MICAH'S PICKS: Maker's Mark, Weller bourbons, Elijah Craig 12-year, Wild Turkey bourbons, Buffalo Trace, Booker's, Basil Hayden's.

SCOTCH WHISKY

PRODUCTION: Scotch whisky is made with barley. Scotch distillers use a process called *malting* to increase the amount of fermentable sugar in the barley grains. In the malting process, the grains are germinated, or allowed to partially grow. The germination process allows enzymes in the seeds to break down complex carbohydrates into fermentable sugars. The grains are then exposed to heat to arrest the germination. In some coastal parts of Scotland, peat is a common fuel source for malting, and peated malts have a pronounced swampy, smoky, iodiney flavor. In Scotland, a whisky can be called a single malt scotch when it is distilled from 100 percent malted barley in pot stills from a single distillery and aged for three years in oak containers. Blended scotch is made from a blend of single malt whisky and other whiskies.

Flavor notes: Styles of scotch can vary wildly, from saline and smoky, to rich and round, to light and floral. Scotch makers may also finish an aged whisky in a second barrel—sherry, rum, and port are common—and this secondary finish can add to the complexity of the final spirit. Scotch is arguably the most flavorful grain distillate, and will show up big on the palate when replacing bourbon or rye in a cocktail.

Pairings: I like to use scotch with vermouth, rich and light sherries, cider, stone fruit, ginger, maple, orange, and bittersweet cordials like Zucca and Campari.

Micah's picks: Mixing uber-expensive single malts is a bit of a waste of money, as many of these distillates stand alone as studies in complexity. On the other hand, a scant ¼ oz. of a (pricey) peaty single malt—like Laphroaig or Lagavulin—can lend a good deal of flavor. Blends are also fine for mixing, such as Johnny Walker Black, Pig's Nose, or Dewar's. Monkey Shoulder, a blend of single malts, is an economical choice for big, rich single malt flavor in a mixed drink.

BRANDY AND OTHER FRUIT DISTILLATES

Production: Brandy is distilled from a fruit wine, most commonly a grape wine. Most styles are aged for at least two years in oak containers. France is the most notable producer of higher quality brandies, and there distillers often blend grape distillates of different ages to make a consistent product from year to year. Apple brandy distilled from hard cider is another common fruit distillate found in many classic cocktails. Some unaged fruit distillates include pisco (made from grapes) and grappa (made from the leftovers of making wine—spent grapes, seeds, and stems).

Flavor notes: French grape brandy (including cognac and armagnac) is one of the more common brandies, and is generally rich and round from barrel aging. The underlying wine base imparts a faint note of tartaric acid (the acid present in grapes and grape wine), and when cognac is subbed for whiskey in a cocktail, you get barrel richness without the grainy notes you would with whiskey. Apple brandy similarly has the roundness of whiskey without the grain notes. Apple brandies frequently have a hint of hard cider, which to me is just a little funky with some basement, bleu cheese flavors. Unaged fruit distillates are particularly aggressive and raw on the palate, and can deliver serious flavor in small and sparing amounts in cocktails.

Pairings: I like to pair cognac and other French brandies with rich aged rum or rye (both classic combos), orange, cider, rich sweet vermouth, absinthe, and baking spices. It's also absolutely perfect in eggnog. Similarly, I like to pair apple brandy with cider, pumpkin, baking spices, rich vermouth, herbs, and herby, bittersweet cordials like Bénédictine and Chartreuse. For my taste, unaged fruit distillates need to be paired in smaller amounts with big flavors, or the rawness of them overwhelms the other ingredients.

Micah's picks: Cognac: Courvoisier cognacs, Paul Giraud cognacs, Pierre Ferrand cognacs. Apple brandy: Calvados Boulard,

Laird's Bonded and Old Apple brandies. Pisco: Pisco Porton. Grappa: Ransom Gewurstraminer.

Sweet

For the longest time, I underestimated how much sugar can do for a drink. I think one of the more common mistakes made by beginning bartenders is skimping on sugar. Your palate will not recognize the mintiness of your mint or the watermeloniness of your watermelon without sugar. Sugar is essential in bringing balance to a cocktail, and you need a decent amount to soften a shot of spirit. I wince and weep when people ask me to make a drink with no or little sugar; the resulting cocktail will inevitably be off-balance. What follows here is a brief discussion of some of the sweet components I reach for the most behind the bar.

SIMPLE SYRUP

The most common sweet ingredient in cocktails is simple syrup. Simple syrup is simply one part water to one part sugar. I measure sugar and water by volume using measuring cups, but some folks like to measure equal weights of sugar and water using a scale. Scales are expensive, and common kitchen scales are frequently not that precise. For me, that makes using scales quickly just a little frustrating. Measuring with measuring cups saves me time, and behind the bar, time is of the essence.

To make simple syrup, add 1 cup water to 1 cup sugar. I use an electric kettle at work to heat the water to get the sugar to dissolve faster. Some folks swear by more complicated sugar-water ratios and heating the bejesus out of the syrup. I've found the simplicity of my method and ratios to work just fine. It's supposed to be simple! Just make sure to cool your syrup before adding it to your cocktail, or the resulting drink will be a tad overdiluted; we'll talk about why in chapter 2.

There are a vast number of riffs on simple syrup. Here are some common ones that are good to know about:

- 2:1 SIMPLE SYRUP (TWO PARTS SUGAR, ONE PART WATER; NEEDS TO BE HEATED TO DISSOLVE THE SUGAR)
- DEMERARA SUGAR SIMPLE SYRUP
- BROWN SUGAR SIMPLE SYRUP
- HONEY SYRUP (ONE PART HONEY, ONE PART WATER)
- AGAVE SYRUP
- CORN SYRUP
- MAPLE SYRUP

You can do a 2:1 riff on all the syrups that have a water component, provided you heat them to give the syrup a uniform texture.

Most importantly, when using simple syrup as the only sweet

component in a cocktail, consider that *it takes ½ to ¾ oz. of 1:1 simple syrup to adequately sweeten a 3 oz. cocktail.*

FLAVORED SYRUPS

There are a myriad of ways of getting flavor into syrups. Let's cover a few, as this will be a big part of incorporating flavors into cocktails. Everyone has a preferred way of making syrup; I try to let the flavor I'm working with guide my approach. Here are a few ways I approach different flavors.

Cooked syrups. This approach works well for dried herbs especially, like peppercorns or baking spices. It's also good for fruits and veggies that need a little heat to open up the flavor, like rhubarb or fresh cranberry in particular. It works less well with flavors that are very delicate or susceptible to getting muddled or mealy. To make a cooked syrup, make a 1:1 simple syrup and heat it in a saucepan with your dried herbs or fruit. Bring it to a boil and simmer for fifteen minutes or so, or until the desired flavor is reached. Strain and refrigerate.

Infused syrups. This is not my favorite technique, but it is one that a lot of folks use. Basically you make a 2:1 syrup, cool the syrup, add fruit, infuse overnight, and strain out the fruit.

Macerated syrups. This is my favorite. In his book *On Food and Cooking,* Harold McGee notes that many of the molecules responsible for the distinctive aromas and flavors of fruit and herbs are heat-sensitive, organic molecules. So, when you expose fresh fruit and herbs to high temperatures, you frequently destroy or lose those essential molecules. The resulting flavors in heated fruit and herb syrups can be cooked, mealy, or muddy. Conversely sugar, also an organic molecule, can be used as a solvent to draw out many of these delicate compounds in the absence of heat, resulting in a richly flavored syrup. Fruits that are good candidates for maceration shouldn't have too much water content and should also have a decent sugar content. Bad candidates: melons, citrus. Good candidates: pineapple, raspberries, strawberries, cherries, peaches, and other stone fruit. This is my go-to ratio for macerated fruit syrups.

> 4 CUPS CHOPPED FRUIT
>
> 2 CUPS SUGAR
>
> 1 CUP WINE

Macerate the fruit with the sugar for a couple of hours, stirring occasionally to get all the fruit coated. Use the wine to help dissolve the remaining sugar. Pulse the syrup a couple of times in a blender (or with an immersion blender) if necessary and strain.

If your fruit is especially ripe and juicy, you can omit the wine. The wine is there mostly to help get the sugar in solution, but it also helps to extend the shelf life of the syrup. A 4:2:1 wine-fortified cordial can last up to two months in the fridge. I omit wine when macerating in-season peaches and strawberries as they are especially juicy and their flavors are particularly ephemeral. I try to use the syrup within a day or two. I would also like to note that I really, really love freshly macerated peaches with bourbon.

Oleo saccharum, or macerated citrus peel syrup. Just as you can draw out the essence of fruit with sugar, you can also draw out the essence and oil of citrus peels with sugar. I usually add the sugar to lemon peels (I find of the big citrus fruits—lemon, lime, orange, and grapefruit—lemon's essence and flavor is mostly truly captured in oleo saccharum), stir the peels up, and wait a couple of hours. The sugar will start to draw the lemon essence out of the peels, and the mixture will start to resemble syrup. If that doesn't happen, use a muddler to push the sugar into the peels to speed up the process. You can add a little water or tea to dissolve the remaining sugar. Here's my usual ratio.

PEELS OF 5 LEMONS

1 CUP SUGAR

1 CUP LIQUID

Making oleo saccharum is a great way to utilize the entire citrus fruit, and we'll see in chapter 3 that this syrup is crucial to making a rich, citrusy classic punch.

OTHER CANDIDATES FOR USE AS A SWEET COMPONENT

Fruit cordials/liqueurs. Many classic cocktails—such as the Margarita and Sidecar—are sweetened with fruit cordials or liqueurs (these two words are used somewhat interchangeably). The essential elements of a cordial/liqueur are: 1) a considerable fruit or nonbitter herb component, 2) a considerable amount of sugar (enough to sweeten a cocktail), and 3) an alcohol percentage that may vary from as low as 17 percent up to 40 percent or greater.

When using a cordial/liqueur, it's useful to ask yourself a couple questions:

SWEETNESS: How sweet is the cordial relative to simple syrup?

BALANCE: What is the ABV? If the cordial/liqueur is adding a significant amount of booze to the drink, you may have to add more sugar or sour/bitter components to compensate for this additional alcohol.

Some of my favorite cordials/liqueurs include Langlois Crème de Mûre, Langlois Crème de Cassis, Pierre Ferrand Dry Curaçao, Cointreau, St. Germain Elderflower Cordial, Belle Paire pear liqueur, and Disaronno amaretto.

BITTERSWEET CORDIALS AND AROMATIZED AND FORTIFIED WINES. Because these are a primary source of the bitter component, we'll cover them in the bitter section that follows. Some of these ingredients do contain significant amounts of sugar, though, and I like to use them in very small amounts to season a drink with just a little sugar, bitter, and an additional dimension of flavor.

Sour/Bitter

Sour/bitter is the least intuitive of our three necessary components. When I'm making batched cocktails for events at the restaurant where I work now, sometimes when I taste them for a quality check I just can't place what's missing. Usually it's acidity, bitterness, or both. Sour/bitter ingredients are essential to a balanced cocktail, as they align our other two ingredients—spirit and sweet—on the palate.

SOUR

To me, citrus is magical. In cooking and in mixing drinks, you need acidity to balance big flavors. A chef's main sources of acidity are vinegar and citrus. Vinegar is a sugar solution that has been metabolized by yeast, and then that yeast excrement is further metabolized by bacteria. In essence, vinegar is yeast poop that has been ingested and then pooped out again by bacteria—not that that makes it any less important or less delicious. Citrus, on the other hand, is nature's pure acid. It represents the earth's willing gift to culinarians: a natural acid that has only to be squeezed gently to bring a world of flavors into crystal-clear focus. I freaking love citrus.

When making drinks, the two most common sources of significant acidity are lemon and lime juice. As with sugar, beginning and home bartenders underestimate the amount of acidity needed to bring balance to a cocktail. Here are a few citrus fruits you might find at the grocery store or in a greenhouse to consider for a sour component:

- LIME
- LEMON
- MEYER LEMON
- KEY LIME
- BERGAMOT
- SEVILLE ORANGE
- GRAPEFRUIT
- ORANGE
- MANDARIN
- CLEMENTINE
- TANGERINE
- CALAMONDIN
- POMELO
- HARDY ORANGE

While many of these are acidic, most do not contain a high enough concentration of citric acid in their juice to adequately bring balance to a cocktail. And while you could use some of the more acidic fruits like Meyer lemons, key limes, or even calamondins as a source of acidity, *it's most practical for home and professional bartenders to use lemon and lime juice as the sour element in a cocktail.* The general rule of thumb is that *it takes about ½ to ¾ oz. of lemon or lime juice to balance a 3 oz. cocktail.* Lime juice *is* just slightly more acidic than lemon juice, and conventional wisdom has been that lime pairs best with neutral and clear spirits, lemon best with aged spirits.

So, lemon or lime? Use your palate! I generally reach for lime when I want really bright flavors, and I've noticed that I use a lot more lime in summer than in winter. Lemon is great with brown spirits, but also great with gin and vodka. Use good sense, our aforementioned rule of thumb, and don't have an existential crisis when reaching for the citrus press.

BITTER

I've had a fraught relationship with the flavor bitter. My mother is a small-town girl from rural North Dakota, and I grew up eating the things that she was raised on: pot roasts, baked chicken, canned and boiled veggies, iceberg lettuce with bottled salad dressing, and a good deal of McDonald's hamburgers. When I heard about cocktail bitters, I was certain that they were not for me. Who likes bitter things? The things I liked most in the world at that time were hamburgers and pizza. How could anyone actively enjoy or seek out that unpleasant, metallic taste?

In short, genetics and evolution are responsible for the perception of the flavor bitter. Our early hominid ancestors were herbivores, and they understood that many toxic plants had a bitter taste. If they could detect a toxic plant via its bitter flavor, they could avoid eating it, and survive. Meanwhile, their bitter-blind neighbors would be munching away to a toxic death. Consequently, the bitter-averse gene became amplified in early hominid populations, and bitter-blind genes dwindled. Early humans subsequently mastered cooking *and* incorporated meat into their diets, thus limiting the necessity of detecting bitter plants. Today both bitter-averse and nonaverse phenotypes exist in human populations, and if you actively dislike bitter, it's likely not your fault.

(This is only part of the discussion on the flavor bitter. Emerging research shows that bitter receptors and bitter foods may contribute to a positive immune response in humans. So is bitter good or bad for us? I'm looking forward to the research that paints a clearer picture of early hominid diners and bartenders.)

I learned to love bitter when I first tasted *good, freshly opened* sweet vermouth. The flavor bitter is a perfect foil to the upfront caramel sweetness and gentle alcohol of sweet vermouth. The bitter finish quickly erases the memory of the initial sweetness and preps your taste buds for another sip. The dance of bitter and sweet is, well, bittersweet! Given the amount of sugar needed to soften a big dram of spirit, bitter is a great foil to bring balance and focus to a shot of sugared alcohol.

In the following section we'll be talking about the most common bitter ingredients: aromatized and fortified wines, bittersweet cordials, and cocktail bitters. We'll look at how to best understand and classify them, discuss what they taste like, and hopefully get some insight into how to Mr.-Potato-Head them effectively.

But first, a quick note on tasting bitter things: Especially with spirit-based bittersweet cordials, the first sip can be overwhelming. When tasting wine, most pros will tell you that having an initial sip will change how your palate perceives the next sip. The pH of your mouth changes as you may start to salivate, and you may be able to detect nuances in subsequent sips not apparent in the first one. So it is when tasting other alcoholic things—especially aggressively bitter things. Let the first sip assault your palate. Then try to detect flavors in subsequent sips.

VERMOUTH AND OTHER A&F WINES

As the names suggests, aromatized and fortified wines (known as A&F wines for short) are fortified with sugar and alcohol, and also flavored with herbs and a bittering agent. Usually a white wine base is used (even for sweet vermouth; the color comes from a caramelized sugar syrup), and the ABV is around 17 percent. The winemaker traditionally chooses a primary bittering agent, and will classify the wine as follows:

BITTERING AGENT	A&F WINE IS CALLED
Wormwood	Vermouth
Cinchona	Quinquina
Gentian (and/or others)	Americano or gentiane

There are a host of other bitter roots, herbs, and barks that have been and are currently used to flavor wines and bittersweet cordials, including: artichoke (used to flavor Cynar), calamus, cardoon (used to flavor Cardamaro), feverfew, horehound (used to flavor horehound candy), licorice root, sarsaparilla, sassafras, and wild cherry bark.

A&F wine styles are regional, muddled by history, and hard to broadly generalize. When picking up a bottle for mixing, getting bogged down in the exact nomenclature, provenance, and bittering agent of the A&F wine is not as important as asking yourself the following:

SWEETNESS: How sweet is the A&F wine?

BITTERNESS: How bitter is it?

COMPLEXITY: What are the dominant flavors? Wine, stone fruit, grass, saline, sulfur, caramel, raisin? Is it light or heavy on the palate?

Having these answers will give you better insight into how to deftly substitute your new ingredient into existing recipes.

Here are the main varieties of vermouth, the most common A&F wine.

DRY: A white-wine-based vermouth made in a French, lower-sugar style. The wine is light, peppery, and sometimes even briny or vegetal. Pairing this style with gin and an olive makes some good sense. It also works well on its own with light, peppery rye whiskies. **MICAH'S PICKS:** Dolin Dry, Ransom Dry, Noilly Prat.

BLANC OR BIANCO: A white-wine-based vermouth made in an Italian style—usually much sweeter and more richly flavored than a dry vermouth. These wines can be viscous and grape-forward, with a nice balance of wormwood on the finish. They are great for adding accents to shaken cocktails with fruit, especially cocktails that are gin-based. **MICAH'S PICKS:** Dolin Blanc, Contratto Bianco, Carpano Bianco.

ROUGE, ROSSO, OR SWEET: This one is tricky. Basically all three labels indicate that you've got a bottle of sweet vermouth. You can expect that wine to be richly flavored, sweetened with caramelized sugar, balanced by a snappy wormwood finish, and made from either a white or red wine base. These vermouths usually have dominant notes of caramel, vanilla, cinnamon, clove, sarsaparilla, dried orange peel, raisins, or dried stone fruit. They are perfect for pairing with aged distillates, especially whiskies. **MICAH'S PICKS:** Carpano Antica, Cocchi Vermouth di Torino, Punt e Mes, Contratto Rosso.

A few other nonvermouth A&F wines I like to keep in my toolbox include Cocchi Americano, Bonal Gentiane Quina, Byrrh quinquina, Lillet Blanc, War and Rust quinquina, Elisir Novasalus, and Cappelletti Aperitivo.

Remember that aromatized and fortified wines, as wines, will over time oxidize and slowly become less tasty than a freshly opened bottle. The sugar content and alcohol fortification do slow this, but the best way to slow it further is to keep your A&F wines in the fridge. After a couple of months opened, repurpose your old A&F wines for cooking.

BITTERSWEET CORDIALS

There's a good reason why the many bottles behind the bar are poorly understood: they're hard to generalize. And in addition, most brands are vague or elusive about what's in the bottle. Consider Green Chartreuse: made from over 130 herbs with a recipe and elaborate protocol that is only known to two monks at a secret distillery in France. I don't think I could name more than 40 herbs, and I know no monks to bro information out of!

This kind of opacity makes these bottles excitingly mysterious for some, and exasperating for others. Fortunately, you have a finely calibrated tool in your toolbox to make heads or tails of these arcane and historical concoctions: your palate! If you have no idea what Becherovka is, pop open the bottle and have a taste. Ask yourself the same questions you would when tasting wine-based bitters, in addition to one more:

> **SWEETNESS:** How sweet is it?
>
> **BITTERNESS:** How bitter is it?
>
> **COMPLEXITY:** What are the dominant flavors? Herbs, mint, smoke, flowers, spices, oranges? Is it rich, light, resinous?
>
> **BALANCE:** What is the ABV?

Most bittersweet cordials are 30 percent ABV or stronger (although some are as low as 11 percent), have a considerable sugar content, and are flavored with a blend of herbs that are complementary to the dominant bittering agent(s). They are themselves delightful to sip and savor while pondering the nuances of the many ingredients from which they are made. And to wax romantic for just a moment, bittersweet cordials remind us of the numerous herbs, medicines, and flavors that humans have valued for centuries—flavors that only survive in the food world in dark bottles behind the bar. It's pretty cool to be the guy that reconnects people to these forgotten things night after night.

Lastly, bittersweet cordials are, in fact, theoretical microstudies of a cocktail: they are a complex balance of spirit, sweet, and bitter. Sipping, appreciating, and understanding them is a great way to gain insight into how to riff on stirred cocktails and add accents to shaken ones.

MICAH'S PICKS: Aperol, Campari, Green Chartreuse, Yellow Chartreuse, absinthe, Fernet Branca, Branca Menta, Bénédictine, Cynar, Luxardo maraschino, Amaro Nonino.

COCKTAIL BITTERS

People always ask me, "What's in all those little bottles?," pointing to the many 4 oz. bottles behind the bar. When I am in the weeds (see appendix) and simply say "Bitters!," the furrow on their brow persists. I dig myself out of the weeds and give a more thoughtful answer:

Cocktail bitters are simply a high-alcohol solution that is infused with a bittering agent (or agents) and other flavors. The solution is in many cases diluted and sweetened. Cocktail bitters differ from bittersweet cordials and A&F wines in that they are used in much more sparing amounts—drops and dashes instead of ounces—and do not add a considerable volume to a drink. In general, they are there to add a hint of bitterness and additional flavor without significantly altering the volume (and balance) of a drink. There are only a handful of cocktails that heavily rely on cocktail bitters as the main source of bitter (the Old Fashioned and the Sazerac in particular), and they are more frequently used in conjunction with other sources of sour or bitter in classic cocktails.

Bitters are easy to make but take some time. If you're curious, check out my basic bitters recipe in the appendix. For a more in-depth discussion on bitters, take a peek at Brad Parson's book *Bitters* or some of the other books in the recommended reading section.

MICAH'S PICKS: Bob's Abbott's, Bob's peppermint, Angostura, Angostura orange, Peychaud's, Amargo Chuncho, Regan's orange.

Before leaving the topic of bitter, let's gloss a few words that might be hanging around ambiguously, some new and some that we've already seen.

> **AROMATIZED AND FORTIFIED (A&F) WINES:** Wines that have been flavored with herbs and a bittering agent (or agents) and fortified with alcohol and sugar, such as vermouths, americanos, quinquinas, or gentianes.
>
> **BITTERSWEET CORDIALS:** Something both aggressively bitter and sweet, generally spirit-based with an ABV of around 30 percent, such as Fernet Branca, Green Chartreuse, or Campari.
>
> **BITTERS:** Usually referring to cocktail bitters, added to cocktails in drops and dashes for flavor and bitterness, such as Angostura or Peychaud's.
>
> **BITTERING AGENT:** A bark, root, or herb that imparts a significant amount of bitterness. The most common bittering agents are wormwood, cinchona, and gentian.
>
> **APERITIF:** Usually something bitter and sweet that has a lower alcohol content (under 20 percent), meant to be consumed at the beginning of a meal. May be wine- or spirit-based.
>
> **DIGESTIF:** Usually something more bitter and sweeter than an aperitif with a higher alcohol content (30 percent or greater), meant to be consumed at the end of a meal. Usually spirit-based.
>
> **AMARO:** Literally "bitter" in Italian. Refers specifically to bittersweet cordials from Italy, and is increasingly used to refer to aperitifs and digestives from other parts of the globe.

2
TOOLS & TECHNIQUES

MAKING A COCKTAIL INVOLVES COMBINING SOMETHING SPIRITOUS, SOMETHING SWEET, AND SOMETHING SOUR or bitter and mixing them. There are two main techniques used for mixing: shaking and stirring. Before we get into the nitty-gritty of which technique works when and what they each do for a drink, we need to introduce the tools and mixing receptacles you'll be using to execute these techniques.

Tools

MIXING GLASSES AND COCKTAIL SHAKERS. When making a drink, you need something to mix it in. Mixing glasses and cocktail shakers are just that. A mixing glass can be as simple as a pint glass, or as ornate as a Japanese crystal mixing glass. I don't use either of these because they are prone to breaking, and they need to be chilled prior to using them (for reasons we'll explain later). I prefer using a pair of metal shakers. I build the drink in the larger bottom shaker, add ice, and when shaking use a smaller metal shaker that fits in the mouth of the larger shaker. Some folks like to use a pint-sized mixing glass as the shaker top, but again, I prefer to use metal as I've broken glasses in my shaker before, and then inadvertently bombarded unsuspecting guests with a shower of staccato profanity. Koriko makes the shaker combo I like to use, and they also make fancy Japanese mixing glasses if you've got money to burn.

BAR SPOONS. I thought bar spoons were silly until I tried stirring a Manhattan with a teaspoon. I made a mess. You really need a spoon with a long stem that protrudes well above the rim of your mixing receptacle, and preferably one that you can spin easily in between your fingers. Use one that feels good in your hand. A locally owned gourmet shop is a good place to pick up a decent bar spoon.

STRAINERS. Bartenders, being the know-it-all, chest-puffing types that they are, love to lecture people on arcana and how they are doing things the wrong way. One popular bartender PSA is the lecture on the julep strainer. A julep strainer is a perforated, scalloped disk with a small handle. Ideally the disk fits snugly in the mouth of the shaker or mixing glass. Ideally. The julep strainer was used in the 1800s not only by the customer but also by the bartender. An iced drink would be served with a julep strainer on top, so that the customer could keep the ice away from his or her teeth, which were likely sensitive due to the low priority of dental hygiene in that day. Bartenders quickly realized the utility of repurposing this same strainer to strain a mixed drink into a chilled glass. The julep strainer gave way to the more practical and evolved Hawthorne strainer, the most common bar strainer. A Hawthorne strainer is a handled, perforated disk that has ears that allow it to sit atop a mixing receptacle and a coil that allows it to both fit snugly in the receptacle and strain out the ice.

If you haven't guessed already, I find antique julep strainers to be beautiful but inefficient, and I prefer using Hawthorne strainers. I nod to history by mentioning them, but do not insist that you feel guilty for not owning one. Nor should you be moonstruck by the mustachioed barkeep who insists that you know about the supremacy of his copper-plated and undoubtedly vintage julep strainer. Hawthorne strainers are used in conjunction with tea strainers at most cocktail bars, for reasons we will cover in the technique section. Koriko makes a Hawthorne strainer with a super-fine coil that is meant to eliminate double straining, but I prefer to use a Hawthorne in combination with a tea strainer for shaken cocktails. I'm fussy like that, I guess.

Peelers. Lots of classic cocktails call for a twist. When I first stepped behind the country club bar, I thought that the twist was just for looks. Usually the precut twists I inherited were pithy (citrus pith can be bitter in an unpleasant way) and sadly just a little dried out. Later in life, I encountered a barkeep wiser than me who freshly cut a thin sliver of citrus and in a single, graceful motion expressed the citrus oil in the peel over the mouth of the cocktail. I could see the oil leave the peel, I could smell it, and that little "garnish" did wonders to brighten and flavor the drink. I was sold. A peeler is a great tool to efficiently get that magical sliver of citrus peel. I swear by Messermeister vegetable peelers, and they hew twists with very little pith.

Muddlers. A muddler is simply a stick or rod of some sort that helps you break up sugar, herbs, or fruit in your glass or shaker. I like using a muddler with an ergonomic handle and larger muddling head. In a pinch, you could use anything in your kitchen with a blunt end to muddle stuff.

Measuring cups/jiggers. One of my first nights behind the banquet bar, a very old, very southern lady said to me, "I havva jigga' vokka-cranburruh." I was certain that she had said something distinctly racist, and later that night went to my boss to decode this strange request. He pulled out a set of jiggers, or measuring cups, and went on to explain that the old lady wanted a shot or jigger of vodka with some cranberry juice. Needless to say I was relieved! My jiggers and measuring cups gathered dust for the many years I worked in a high-volume bar, and I only dusted them off when I got serious about making precise and consistent cocktails.

Do you need to measure your ingredients? In a pinch, no. As a matter of habit, yes. Measuring your ingredients will make your drinks more consistent and balanced, and give you greater insight into how to manipulate ingredients when Mr.-Potato-Heading your way to new creations. I like to use a single measuring cup that can measure all common volumes as opposed to a set of jiggers. It saves me time and

space, and I'm too darn sensible to argue with that—especially on a busy night.

GLASSWARE. Once you've mixed a drink, you need a glass to strain it into. I am not overly opinionated about which drinks go in which glasses in a broad sense. I do insist that my staff serves Old Fashioneds in short tumblers and Manhattans in cocktail coupes for consistency's sake. Use good sense when selecting glassware. The glassware featured in this book is one of my few vices; I love to collect antique glassware, and I did splurge on some of the coupes featured in the photographs. Here are a few staple cocktail glasses that are worth knowing about and having in your home bar.

- COCKTAIL COUPES
- CHAMPAGNE FLUTES
- COLLINS GLASSES
- TUMBLERS/ROCKS GLASSES

Techniques

The following section contains the core technical knowledge you'll need to properly create great cocktails. My experience has been that getting technical is where I lose most folks, but having a baseline of technical knowledge is crucial to getting good results. The information here represents the bare minimum of knowledge you need to produce professional-quality cocktails. If the technique section really floats your boat, I'd recommend reading *The Bar Book* by Jeffrey Morgenthaler, and then *Liquid Intelligence* by Dave Arnold. Their insights and data have paved the way for a quick read on technique here. Let's dive in.

ICE, CHILLING, AND DILUTION

When I first started bartending, I remember hearing members at the club shouting "Don't bruise the gin!" at my boss when he was mak-

ing a Martini. *Bruise the gin?* What could that possibly mean? In the late 1990s, food science and food infotainment was not the multi-million-dollar industry it is today, and the internet was still young. To find out what this meant, I inevitably had to sheepishly ask the self-important bartenders of the day, who relied nearly exclusively on patron ignorance to hide how little they actually knew. "Gin would be bruised and ruined if you shook it, of course!" they said. What about other gin cocktails that are shaken? What about a Gimlet? Is the gin ruined then? I was confused. What was lacking from the conversation was the vocabulary that follows here, and a recognition of the Fundamental Law of Chilled Drinks, furnished by Dave Arnold:

> THERE IS NO CHILLING
> WITHOUT DILUTION, AND
> THERE IS NO DILUTION
> WITHOUT CHILLING.

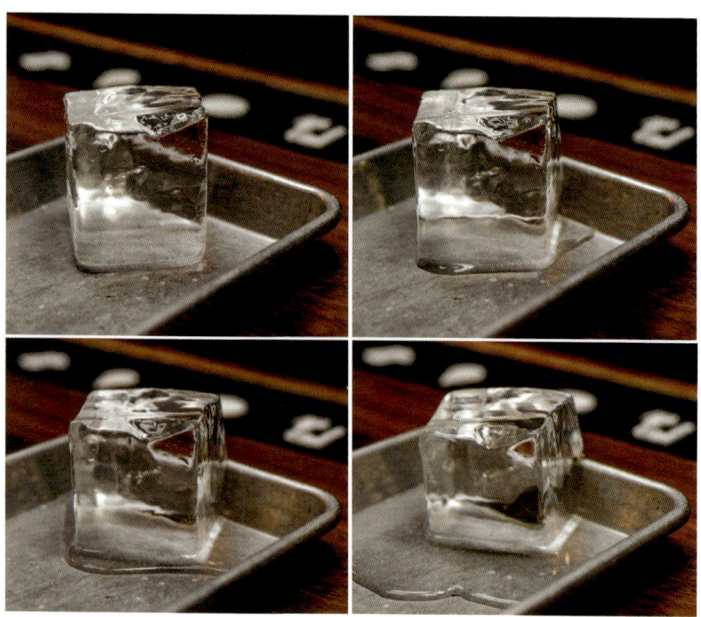

When I teach cocktail classes, I like to use a visual aid to help people understand this concept. Take an ice cube and put it on a plate. Wait a minute. What has happened in that minute? The ice has melted so there's a little water spreading out on the plate, but also the plate has gotten colder. The plate cannot get cold without the ice melting, and the ice cube can't melt without cooling the plate. In other words, *there is a direct relationship between the amount of chilling and how much dilution comes off of our ice.* Why is this important? Because our two main techniques—shaking and stirring—vary with regard to how much dilution occurs in each. Necessarily, according to our fundamental law, they will produce different final temperatures that reflect different degrees of dilution. These techniques also impart different qualities to the resulting drink, which we'll discuss below.

A quick note on tools before we proceed: We just agreed that as ice melts on the plate, the plate gets colder. Optimally, we don't want to have the plate, so to speak, in our shaker. That is, we don't want to add anything extra in our shaker that ice has to chill, as that chilling will come with extra dilution. Fancy mixing glasses have that effect unless they are prechilled—our ice has to do work to chill a room-temperature mixing glass, and that comes at the expense of additional dilution. Prechilling takes time, and behind the bar, time, again, is of the essence. I like to use metal shakers, which have very low thermal absorption (ice does minimal work to chill them). Mixing glasses *are* beautiful, and sometimes aesthetics do get the best of me. When they do, I make sure to chill the mixing glass before making a Manhattan.

SHAKING

When you shake a drink, the ice and the cocktail are combined in a shaker and placed in an intensely turbulent environment. The interaction of the ice and cocktail is vigorous, and consequently the drink is both more diluted and more chilled as compared to stirring. To get the right degree of chilling and dilution, shake for about twelve seconds. The final temperature of a shaken drink should be close to 20° F, well below the freezing point of water. This is a thermodynamic peculiarity of alcohol-water solutions, and usually people's eyes glaze over when I start talking about the science. It's outside the scope of most folks' interest, but should nonetheless be on your radar and at least inspire awe if not curiosity.

The act of shaking also imparts some significant qualitative effects. A shaken drink is significantly aerated and lighter on the palate. Shaking also helps to emulsify any thick or pulpy ingredients. *In general, shaking is the preferred technique when you have a cocktail with any fruit juice or thicker ingredients; stirring is preferred with cocktails that have no juice.*

How to execute: To shake properly, load your ingredients into the larger tin, *then add ice* (you want to uniformly chill and dilute your ingredients!). Insert the smaller shaker bottom-up into the larger shaker, give it a tap with your palm to get a good seal, and shake with both hands for about twelve seconds. When you're done shaking, the tins will be stuck together. Using the butt of your hand, give the shaker another tap on the side where the two tins meet. Don't despair if they don't come apart immediately. As the volume of air inside the shaker gets colder it shrinks, and you get just a bit of a vacuum effect between the two tins. As a result, you'll need a little elbow grease to separate them. Place a Hawthorne strainer coil-side down in the mouth of the shaker. Hold a tea strainer in your other hand and double strain the cocktail into a chilled cocktail glass. Double straining removes the little ice chips that form in the turbulent environment of shaking. At the end of shaking for twelve seconds, we've reached our target temperature and dilution, and we want to remove any small bits of ice that might affect the final dilution of the cocktail.

DRY SHAKING, OR HOW TO PROPERLY TREAT AN EGG WHITE. Several classic cocktails—including the Whiskey Sour—call for an egg white. When I first started making drinks, I thought that sounded really gross. As it turns out, history is right and I was wrong: when done properly, dry shaking a cocktail with an egg white is a fantastic way to add lightness, roundness, and a rich, airy mouth feel. An egg white can also help to emulsify ingredients that contain fat or are pulpy or particulate. If you make a drink and the ingredients settle, coagulate, or separate, you can usually solve this problem by using an egg white.

To separate a white from a yolk, get two clean containers, one for yolks and one for whites. Crack an egg and catch the yolk between your fingers, letting the white fall into a clean container below. At home I keep the yolks to make aioli or I give them to my dogs. Use clean hands and fresh eggs to avoid any food-borne illness. I toss or repurpose surplus whites after a day just to be on the safe side. A single cocktail usually calls for around half an ounce of egg white or half of the white of a single large egg.

How to execute: Load your ingredients into a large metal shaker, adding the egg white last. Place the smaller metal shaker bottom-up into the mouth of the larger shaker, and give the top shaker a good tap with the palm of your hand to ensure a good seal. Shake with two hands for about fifteen seconds. The tins will come apart easily, as you haven't changed the temperature of the cocktail or the air in the shaker. Add ice and shake the cocktail a second time as outlined above.

STIRRING

Stirring is a more elegant technique compared to shaking. Originally, stirring was introduced to mitigate the gauche flamboyance of bartenders in late 1800s, who were no doubt eager to emulate the flair and legitimate showmanship of Jerry Thomas and his famous Blue Blazer cocktail—a cocktail that was lit on fire and then thrown deftly between two open-mouthed mixing tankards. Stirring, on the other hand, creates a gentle and graceful spinning environment where ice and cocktail meet, and the resulting drink is not as chilled, not as diluted, not turbulently aerated, and not emulsified in any way.

Two quick anecdotes: One of my favorite guilty pleasures is Rumpleminze peppermint schnapps, right from the freezer. In the freezer, my beloved Rumples is quite viscous, and much of the burn of the schnapps (it's 50 percent ABV) is masked by the almost syrup-like texture it has when it is subzero. This is not the temperature you want for your Manhattan. You want it to be cold, but not subzero, not viscous-from-the-freezer cold. Most folks agree that the optimal temperature and dilution of a stirred cocktail occurs at a final temperature of around or just under 32° F. Any colder and you really start to lose some of the flavor of the drink. Good for masking the burn of Rumples, bad with Manhattans.

Second, have you ever had (the misfortune of having) a shaken Manhattan? Indeed I have, and it was remarkable to me how much the extra chilling, dilution, and aeration—aeration especially—changed how the drink felt on the palate. All that to say, the texture of a stirred drink should be smooth—*silky* is a word commonly used—with no aeration and less dilution, and it shouldn't be Rumples-from-the-freezer cold.

> ***How to execute:*** To stir properly, load your ingredients into the shaker or mixing glass, *then add ice* (remember, you want to uniformly chill and dilute your ingredients!). Stir gently with a bar spoon, spinning the spoon between your thumb and your index and middle fingers. Dave Arnold's research shows that an overwhelming majority of the chilling possible in a stirred cocktail occurs in the first

thirty seconds of stirring, so for me that is the point of diminishing returns. It's also when the drink lands right around or under 32° F. If you stir for an additional minute and a half, you can get your cocktail just a couple degrees colder (and more diluted), but that's three times as long to make one drink. I like to feel the side of my metal shaker with my hand to get an idea of how the dilution and chilling is going. I can tell when the side of the shaker is getting near ice-cold, and then I know I'm just about done stirring. After stirring, use a Hawthorne strainer (or a julep strainer if you like) to strain your drink into a chilled cocktail glass.

So, when making drinks at home, when do you shake and when do you stir? You shake when you have juice or thicker ingredients that need to be emulsified, and when you want aeration and greater chilling and dilution. You stir when you have no juice, when you want a silky mouth feel, and when you want no aeration with less chilling and dilution. Let's line those things up and review the quantitative and qualitative differences the two techniques yield.

	SHAKING	STIRRING
Dilution	More	Less
Chilling	Around 20° F	Around 32° F
Emulsification	Yes	No
Aeration	Yes	No
Time to execute	About twelve seconds	About thirty seconds
Example	Daiquiri	Manhattan

MAKING FANCY CLEAR ICE BLOCKS

Before leaving the topic of chilling, dilution, and ice, let's talk about an easy trick for your next party: making a clear block of ice. Water will not freeze into clear blocks of ice for a couple of simple reasons that have more complicated science behind them: 1) the water has too much dissolved gas or particulate matter in it, and 2) ice crystals begin forming from multiple sides of the container, trapping gas inside. How do you reduce dissolved gas and particulates and get ice to form from only direction? By adding filtered, boiled water to an insulated cooler, and putting the cooler in the freezer. The filtering gets the particulates, the boiling reduces gases, and the insulated cooler exposes only one side of the water to cold, ensuring top-down freezing. As the water gets colder and colder, ice crystals will form near the surface of the water. As the network of crystals grows deeper into the water below, it acts as a natural filter that pushes any gas or particulate matter out of the forming ice block. As we talked about in chapter 1, ice appeared in cocktails in the early 1800s—long before the advent of commercial refrigerators and at a time when municipal water was not widely potable. This was only possible because ice formed in (unpolluted) freshwater lakes is naturally pure.

To make a block of clear ice, put your cooler of filtered, boiled water in the freezer for at least twenty-four hours. Pull the cooler out before the block freezes through. If it freezes through, the bottom inch of the block will be cloudy, but you can trim that off as outlined in the tips below.

- Turn your block out over a clean sink or sheet pan that can catch any water that is unfrozen.
- Allow your block to rest for a half hour or so, so that it can temper and adjust to room temperature. An untempered block will have a cloudy appearance, and it will shatter if you attempt to cut it.
- Set the block where it won't easily slip, like on a clean kitchen towel on a flat surface.
- Using another clean kitchen towel, hold the block firmly with your nondominant hand. With your dominant hand, use a serrated knife to score the ice block, and then score the block again on the opposite side.
- Insert your knife into the first scored groove, and use a mallet to gently tap the back of your knife. A scored and tempered clear block should cleave cleanly.
- Put a clean towel over your ice block between cuts to prolong its life.

→ Ice is slippery! Be sure that the block is not on a slippery surface, and don't forget to use a clean towel to hold the block steady when cutting. And if you're having more than a Manhattan or two that evening, it's best to cut the block while your hand-eye coordination is at its best. ER visits suck.

Ice blocks are an inexpensive party trick if you've got a cooler handy, and you can process one with reasonable proficiency after making a block or two. And because the target temperature of a stirred cocktail is 32° F, serving it on a large cube (also at 32° F) ensures the right temperature for the life of the drink—provided you don't take hours to drink it.

Big, clear cubes are beautiful, and they're an easy way to impress guests at your next cocktail party. Besides that, clear ice is proof of purity—it visually demonstrates the lack of dissolved gas and particulates. If you think about a shaken or stirred cocktail having as much as 30 percent of its final volume coming from the ice in the shaker, an argument could be made for using clear ice for all shaken and stirred cocktails. Regular freezer ice can make great drinks, but just be sure not to have too much stinky stuff in your freezer, or it will show up in your ice and your cocktails. Much to my embarrassment, my wife has called me out for making her a shrimpy Manhattan with stinky ice from our freezer at home.

OTHER TECHNIQUES

MUDDLING

Muddling is a good way to get flavor into a drink on the fly, and it's a preferred technique with fresh herbs. Generally speaking, herbs with softer leaves (basil and mint especially) only need to be bruised with a muddler. Over-muddling these herbs can leave grassy off-flavors. In my experience, herbs with stiffer leaves and stems (rosemary, thyme, or lemon verbena, for example) need to be muddled a bit more to coax out their flavor. In general, if you aren't happy with the herb flavor, use more herbs instead of muddling them into a paste. Also, consider that shaking herbs or fruit in a shaker with ice will act to additionally muddle those ingredients. When using citrus, over-muddling—especially the pith in the peel—can lead to an unpleasantly bitter drink.

RINSING

Many classic cocktails—like the Corpse Reviver No. 2, the Sazerac, or the Improved Whiskey Cocktail—call for an absinthe-rinsed glass. Why would you rinse a glass rather than add the ingredient to your shaker? Good question. Absinthe is incredibly potent. Rather than risk adding too much to a cocktail (sometimes even ⅛ oz. or a bar spoon can overwhelm a drink), bartenders have historically preferred to put a scant ¼ oz. in a glass, swirl it around, and then dump it out. Other potent ingredients can be treated similarly, especially if you fear that adding a full ¼ oz. will overwhelm your drink. Since modern absinthe is especially expensive, you can use a plant mister or a food-grade spray bottle to coat your glass with minimal waste.

INFUSIONS

Another way to get flavor into your shaker is by infusing spirits, bittersweet cordials, or A&F wines with fruit or herbs. In a best-case scenario, the ethanol extracts the organic molecules that make up the essence of the fruit or herb. In a worst-case scenario, the infusion is weak, the flavors muddy, or the infusion pulls out unpleasant, astringently bitter flavors. For me, there are only a few instances where I like using infusions. Here are my tips.

- → Don't over-infuse. Strawberries left in a bottle of gin for six months will inevitably be unpleasant and muddy. Fresh ingredients quickly yield their flavor, so taste your infusion daily to know when to separate your booze from your infusion stuff.

- → Use big flavors for infusions, and avoid weak ones. Flavors that are spicy, tannic, or oily are good candidates for infusions. Big: spicy or dried peppers, dried fruit, baking spices, tea, coffee, citrus peel, spruce tips. Weak: watermelons and other watery melons, soft herbs like basil. For weaker flavors, use more of the flavoring agent, not a longer infusion time.

- → Note your quantity of ingredients and time of infusion for future reference. A little data goes a long way.

- → Keep infusions refrigerated for maximum shelf life.

USING LENGTHENERS

Sometimes when I've made a cocktail, I find it's just a little too potent or concentrated. A great way to solve this problem is to add a lengthener. Lengtheners are anything low- or nonalcoholic that can stretch a concentrated drink over a larger volume, while also adding flavor. Here are a few common lengtheners:

> FRUIT JUICE
>
> SODA
>
> TEA
>
> WINE
>
> BEER
>
> SHERRIES, PORTS, AND OTHER FORTIFIED WINES
>
> AROMATIZED AND FORTIFIED WINES (adds bitter)

The most common lengthener is undoubtedly fruit juice, and 1 to 2 oz. of the season's freshest juice can do wonders for an ordinary Daiquiri. In the summer I love adding watermelon juice to Daiquiris, Margaritas, and Gimlets. That extra length in a cocktail is a real crowd-pleaser with folks who don't drink very much. At family reunions, my liquor-averse relatives don't mind having a Watermelon Margarita or two.

JUICING

Here are a few tips on how to get the best juice, either for lengtheners or for our primary sour components, lemon and lime.

CITRUS. As much as you are able, use fresh citrus juice. Freshly squeezed juices make a tremendous difference in the flavor of a cocktail. For our requisite sour ingredients lemon and lime, I'd recommend an enamel lemon squeezer. For larger citrus fruits like orange, grapefruit, or pomelo, a manual citrus press or one with a motorized

reamer is a good choice. Breville makes a good motorized reamer, the Citrus Press 800CPXL, and I use this machine every day at work for lemons, limes, oranges, and grapefruit.

HARD FRUITS. To juice things like beets, carrots, ginger, sweet potatoes, apples, pears, or other harder fruits, I'd recommend using a centrifugal juicer. The flavors you get from fresh juice are vibrant but very shelf-unstable. They will oxidize pretty quickly, so juice just prior to mixing for optimal flavor.

SOFT FRUITS. You can also run these through a centrifugal juicer (just make sure to get the pits and hard seeds out), or you can use an immersion blender to mix the fruit and then strain it. My immersion blender comes in handy when juicing watermelon, cantaloupe, and other juicy summer melons. For fruit with a higher sugar content (peaches are a prime example), consider macerating them to make a rich syrup and using them as your sweet component.

GARNISHES

Indulge me finally on a technical discussion of garnishes. Some garnishes are functional and some are aesthetic, and most drinks have a preferred garnish. Optimally a good garnish should be both functional and aesthetic, enhancing both the flavor and the visual appeal of a cocktail. Here are few common garnishes and some guidelines for their construction.

Wedges. Wedges are the inglorious workhorses of garnishes. Whereas a perfectly uniform, circular lime wheel looks beautiful in a photo of a gin and tonic, a wedge is what you really want if you need a squeeze of lime without making your hands a total mess. Good knives are a necessity for cooking and cocktails, and I'd recommend hewing your citrus with a sharp knife with a six-inch blade (at least) to yield regular, not jagged or sawed-looking cuts. Remember, functional *and* aesthetic.

Wheels. If you've already used our sound theoretical approach to make a balanced cocktail, a wheel (a cut right through the equator of a lemon or lime) is a nice way to garnish a drink without changing the flavor. These are difficult to cut evenly, so don't get super stressed if your wheel isn't perfectly cut the first time out of the gate.

Half- and quarter-wheels. I like using orange half-wheels and grapefruit quarter-wheels, as orange and grapefruit wedges look big and clunky on the rim of a glass. Very few cocktails are enhanced by a few drops of orange or grapefruit juice, so I opt for wheels over wedges with these fruits.

Twists. This is the perfect example of the functional and aesthetic garnish. Take a vegetable peeler and peel a strip longitudinally (from end to end) out of a piece of citrus, getting as little white pith as possible. Hold the strip in both hands with the peel side down, and squeeze the peel over the face of the drink in one motion. Rim the glass with the peel side of the strip, then curl it into a twist and perch it on the lip of the glass. Citrus oil works wonderfully to perfume a cocktail and brings an additional dimension of brightness, especially with stirred cocktails.

Flavored rims. Rimming a cocktail glass is a good way to introduce a flavor without having to integrate that flavor with your other cocktail ingredients. To do this, moisten the outside lip of a cocktail glass with a wedge of citrus. Spread your rimming ingredient on a small plate. Gently press the moistened lip into the rimming ingredient, and wipe off any excess with a clean napkin. I usually only

rim half of a glass with a rimming ingredient, just so folks can have the option of taking or leaving that flavor.

HERBS. Herbs can make great functional and aesthetic garnishes, as they give your nose something to brush up against and smell, enhancing the olfactory aspect of a drink, and they can also look nice. They *can* look nice. Use fresh, fragrant, good-looking herbs for garnishes. Please, please, please don't use ugly, dying, or nonfragrant herbs. Some people loudly spank their garnishes with a grandiose clap to "wake the herbs." I don't do that because I think it makes me look like a peacocking hipster. I just give them a little squeeze or a tap on an open palm, and I think that does the trick without drawing too much attention to myself.

GARNISHING EGG-WHITE COCKTAILS

If you've properly shaken a cocktail with egg white, it will have a nice quarter inch or more of frothy head sitting on top of the drink, like a perfect meringue pillow. This pillow allows for a little innovation when it comes to garnishing egg-white cocktails. Common garnishes include dropping bitters into the meringued head and making fun designs, not unlike the latte artwork common at fancy coffee shops (see the Whiskey Sour in chapter 3 for an example). You can also float droplets of oil or heavier things like herbs or even sprinkles. I like to garnish fruity egg-white cocktails like the Clover Club (see chapter 3 again) with sprinkles made from bittersweet cordials, for a pop of texture and bitter plus a hint of sweet.

3

STIRRED & SHAKEN COCKTAILS

I N CHAPTER 1, WE LAID THE THEORETICAL FRAMEWORK OF SPIRIT, SWEET, AND SOUR/BITTER, AND WE INTRODUCED THE Mr. Potato Head method of recipe manipulation. In chapter 2, we introduced our essential tools and our two core techniques, shaking and stirring. In this chapter, we'll examine an archetypal cocktail in each of these categories, and we'll relate all of the classic and original drinks included here back to those basic archetypes. Please don't misunderstand me when I use the word "archetype"—I'm not claiming that the following cocktail archetypes are the most ancient, most delicious, or most fancy classic cocktails around. The archetype is a teaching tool. It is a point of reference for creating successful drinks. The following archetypes create the Mr. Potato Head scaffold that allows you to plug in and manipulate your requisite ingredients. Let's get mixing!

Manhattan

Stirred cocktail archetype

2 OZ. BULLEIT RYE WHISKEY
1 OZ. CARPANO ANTICA SWEET VERMOUTH
4 DROPS BOB'S ABBOTT'S BITTERS

Stir (see chapter 2) and serve in a chilled cocktail coupe. Garnish with a cherry.

While the exact date of the creation of the Manhattan is unknown, American bartenders were making Manhattans as early as the 1880s. The simple and delicious combination of whiskey with vermouth is a culinary no-brainer, and was likely independently reasoned to by several bartenders of the day. Understanding why the Manhattan works and the structure of the drink is key to mastering stirred cocktails. For the purposes of manipulating the archetype, let's classify our ingredients:

Rye whiskey	Spirit
Sweet vermouth	Sweet, bitter
Bitters	Bitter, additional flavor complexity

The ratios listed in the recipe above can be edged a little up or down, but our ideal ratio for stirred cocktails is about 2 total oz. spirit to about 1 total oz. bittersweet cordial or A&F wine. (The bitters add an optional flavor accent and won't figure in our basic scaffolding for drinks based on the Manhattan.) Please get to know these proportions and introduce them to your palate. You may find that tweaking them just a little jibes best with how you prefer your cocktails. With my vanilla upbringing, it may come as little surprise that I like my cocktails just a hair on the sweet side.

Tasting notes: This cocktail tastes like delicious, boozy cinnamon raisin bread. Bulleit is a rich rye, Carpano Antica is a raisiny, caramel-sweet vermouth with a big note of vanilla, and Bob's Abbott's bitters are heavy with clove and tonka bean (the bean looks like a large, elongated raisin and has notes of coffee, chocolate, and clove). The vermouth and bitters really fill out the rye whiskey, and the grainy, bready notes of the whiskey play nicely with the caramel sweetness and spice in the vermouth and bitters. In this basic formula of 2–1–dash, any substitution of rye for rye, vermouth for vermouth, or bitters for bitters will have a big effect on the final product. As such, the Manhattan is a good vehicle for exploring the nuances of whiskies, vermouths, and bitters.

Martini

Stirred classic

2 OZ. JUNIPERO GIN
1 OZ. DOLIN DRY VERMOUTH

Stir and serve in a chilled cocktail coupe. Garnish with a lemon twist (see chapter 2).

DOES THE STRUCTURE LOOK FAMILIAR? We simply took the Manhattan format and substituted gin for rye and dry vermouth for sweet vermouth.

2 oz. rye (spirit)	→	2 oz. gin (spirit)
1 oz. sweet vermouth (sweet, bitter)	→	1 oz. dry vermouth (sweet, bitter)

TASTING NOTES: This is a successful cocktail but very different from the Manhattan. The winey vermouth, peppery and bitter with just a hint of sweetness, balances and lengthens the heavy juniper notes in a healthy 2 oz. jigger of gin. It makes a good deal of sense to pair this dry, peppery vermouth with olives, but a lemon twist will also complement and brighten the drink. Like the Manhattan, the Martini is a good scaffold to explore the nuances of different gins and vermouths.

Corpse Reviver No. 1

Stirred classic

- 1 OZ. CALVADOS BOULARD
- 1 OZ. COURVOISIER VSOP COGNAC
- 1 OZ. COCCHI VERMOUTH DI TORINO SWEET VERMOUTH
- 1 DASH ANGOSTURA BITTERS

Stir and serve in a chilled cocktail coupe. Garnish with a cherry.

ARE YOU SEEING A PATTERN YET? In this cocktail, the 2 oz. of rye we started with in our Manhattan cocktail is split into two different spirits, and we keep the sweet vermouth and a dash of bitters. The idea of splitting the spirit portion of a drink into two different distillates is something that we'll see again and again. It's a cool way to add complexity to a drink.

2 oz. rye (spirit)	→	1 oz. apple brandy 1 oz. cognac (spirit)
1 oz. sweet vermouth (sweet, bitter)	→	1 oz. sweet vermouth (sweet, bitter)
		Angostura bitters (bitter, complexity)

TASTING NOTES: On first glance you might dismiss this as being too similar to a Manhattan, but the fruit distillates used in place of the rye eliminate the grain and bread notes in the drink and replace them with faint cider and wine barrel notes. It's a nice demonstration of how substituting barrel-aged distillates of different provenance can have a significant impact on the final product. The Corpse Reviver No. 1 is a Manhattan minus the bread sub fruit.

Vieux Carré

Stirred classic

¾ OZ. PIKESVILLE 110 RYE WHISKEY
¾ OZ. COURVOISIER VSOP COGNAC
¾ OZ. CARPANO ANTICA SWEET VERMOUTH
¼ OZ. BÉNÉDICTINE
3 DASHES PEYCHAUD'S BITTERS
3 DASHES ANGOSTURA BITTERS

Stir and serve in a tumbler with a single large ice cube (see chapter 2). Garnish with a lemon twist.

This time we've taken the 2 oz. of rye present in our Manhattan and tweaked that down to 1½ oz. total volume of spirit. As in the Corpse Reviver No. 1, we've split that 1½ oz. into two ¾ oz. portions, one of rye and one of cognac. The sweet vermouth component remains but is split into two portions, ¾ oz. sweet vermouth and ¼ oz. Bénédictine. Let's diagram that out:

2 oz. rye (spirit)	→	¾ oz. rye ¾ oz. cognac (spirit)
1 oz. sweet vermouth (sweet, bitter)	→	¾ oz. sweet vermouth ¼ oz. Bénédictine (sweet, bitter)
		Angostura bitters Peychaud's bitters (bitter, complexity)

We also add just a few more dashes of cocktail bitters for complexity and bitter balance. This is a classic New Orleans cocktail, and Peychaud's bitters are called for in most stirred New Orleans cocktails that feature aged distillates.

Tasting notes: This is another near-approximation of a Manhattan. It's not as bready as a Manhattan, and the higher bitter-to-spirit ratio makes this cocktail less boozy, more bitter, and a bit more herby with the herbal bittersweet cordial Bénédictine. This is a great cocktail to have before or after a meal.

Widow's Kiss

Stirred classic

1½ OZ. LAIRD'S OLD APPLE BRANDY
¾ OZ. YELLOW CHARTREUSE
¾ OZ. BÉNÉDICTINE
1 DASH ANGOSTURA BITTERS

Stir and serve in a chilled cocktail coupe. Garnish with a cherry.

It all comes back to our basic formula of about 2 oz. spirit to about 1 oz. bittersweet cordial or A&F wine. Here we dial down the spirit just a hair and bump up our bittersweet portion just a bit.

2 oz. rye (spirit)	→	1½ oz. apple brandy (spirit)
1 oz. sweet vermouth (sweet, bitter)	→	¾ oz. Yellow Chartreuse ¾ oz. Bénédictine (sweet, bitter)
		Angostura bitters (bitter, complexity)

Part of the reason for dialing back the spirit is because the bittersweet cordials that carry our sweet and bitter components—Yellow Chartreuse and Bénédictine—are both 40 percent ABV, as opposed to around 17 percent ABV for the vermouth in the Manhattan. We bump up the bittersweet proportions here to give us just a little more sugar and bitter to mask the fact that there is nothing low-ABV in this cocktail.

Tasting notes: I love this cocktail: rich, boozy, and sweet, with balance coming from herbal bittersweet cordials. Yellow Chartreuse and Bénédictine are delightfully herbal, honey-rich, and bitter, and provide a perfect foil to a rich apple brandy. This cocktail is very much an herbal, cider-spirit Manhattan riff.

Martinez

Stirred classic

1½ OZ. RANSOM OLD TOM GIN
1½ OZ. PUNT E MES SWEET VERMOUTH
¼ OZ. LUXARDO MARASCHINO
1 DASH ANGOSTURA BITTERS

Stir and serve in a chilled cocktail coupe. Garnish with an orange twist.

THE MARTINEZ IS a classic that is both a historical and a cognitive bridge between the Manhattan and the Martini. It is a mix of Old Tom gin (a gin that may be sweetened and/or aged, if you recall from chapter 1) and *sweet* vermouth, with a scant ¼ oz. of maraschino liqueur and a dash of cocktail bitters. We bumped down the spirit quantity and bumped up the vermouth and bitters.

2 oz. rye (spirit)	→	1½ oz. Old Tom gin (spirit)
1 oz. sweet vermouth (sweet, bitter)	→	1½ oz. sweet vermouth ¼ oz. Luxardo maraschino (sweet, bitter)
		Angostura bitters (bitter, complexity)

TASTING NOTES: You would not expect a gin drink to be this deep, dark, floral, spicy, and delicious. Ransom Old Tom is a barrel-aged gin with heavy juniper and spice notes that pairs perfectly with Punt e Mes, a raisiny, resinous sweet vermouth with hints of stone fruit. On its own maraschino liqueur can be unpleasantly soapy, but in ⅛ and ¼ oz. amounts it can add pleasant floral and fruity notes to cocktails, both stirred and shaken. The orange twist brings brightness that complements the elements of spice and dark fruit in the cocktail.

Sazerac

Stirred classic

1¾ OZ. PAUL GIRAUD VSOP COGNAC
½ OZ. SIMPLE SYRUP
3 DASHES PEYCHAUD'S BITTERS
2 DASHES ANGOSTURA BITTERS
ABSINTHE RINSE

Stir and serve in a tumbler with an absinthe rinse (see chapter 2). Garnish with a lemon twist.

This is an ancient "cock-tail," a New Orleans variation of the Old Fashioned that was popular in the early 1800s. Rye eventually replaced the cognac brandy called for in the original recipe when *Phylloxera* aphids destroyed grapevine rootstocks in Europe, making French brandy globally scarce in the later part of the 1800s. Rye works just fine in a Sazerac, but I prefer the grainless version with cognac a little better. This is one of the few cocktails where cocktail bitters, along with a potently bitter absinthe rinse, are sufficient to foil the sweetened booze base.

2 oz. rye (spirit)	→	1¾ oz. cognac (spirit)
1 oz. sweet vermouth (sweet, bitter)	→	½ oz. simple syrup (sweet) Angostura bitters Peychaud's bitters Absinthe (bitter, complexity)

Tasting notes: This is one of my favorite cocktails of all time. It's largely responsible for making me curious about stirred cocktails. The Sazerac tastes like perfectly sweet, bitter-balanced brandy candy. A cocktail this simple is a perfect illustration of how our theoretical formula of spirit-sweet-sour/bitter can yield something so integrated and yummy out of seemingly disparate ingredients. Please do yourself a favor and make one of these. It will make you want to master stirred cocktails.

Negroni

Stirred classic

- 1 OZ. TANQUERAY GIN
- 1 OZ. CARPANO ANTICA SWEET VERMOUTH
- 1 OZ. CAMPARI

Stir and serve in a chilled cocktail coupe. Garnish with an orange twist.

This is our biggest deviation from our stirred archetype, but it's easy to see how this recipe relates to the Manhattan. The Negroni is structured like a fifty-fifty Manhattan, with an additional measure of a bittersweet cordial. Specifically, we bump down the spirit to 1 oz., keep our sweet vermouth at 1 oz., and add an equal 1 oz. measure of Campari. With vermouth (17 percent ABV) and Campari (24 percent ABV) making up two-thirds of the (prediluted) volume of the drink, the Negroni is a lower ABV stirred cocktail. It's perfect for before or after dinner, or on a sunny afternoon on the patio.

2 oz. rye (spirit)	→	1 oz. gin (spirit)
1 oz. sweet vermouth (sweet, bitter)	→	1 oz. sweet vermouth (sweet, bitter)
		1 oz. Campari (sweet, bitter)

Take note! This ratio of equal parts spirit-vermouth-bittersweet cordial pops up again and again in successful classic and original stirred cocktails. The Negroni is the second most important stirred cocktail to master!

Tasting notes: I like to pair the assertive bitterness of Campari with a rich sweet vermouth like Carpano Antica. And I love juniper-heavy gins, so Tanqueray is what I generally reach for. Not being the biggest fan of Campari, I'm amazed how much I like how it tastes in the presence of good vermouth and gin. The orange twist is a bright foil to the sweetness of the vermouth and Campari. The Negroni is indeed a perfect cocktail, and has classic variations where bourbon subs for gin (a Boulevardier) and where rye does likewise (an Old Pal). Just about every fancy bartender has his or her own signature riff on a Negroni.

Bijou

Stirred classic

1 OZ. BOMBAY GIN
1 OZ. CARPANO ANTICA SWEET VERMOUTH
1 OZ. GREEN CHARTREUSE
2 DASHES ANGOSTURA ORANGE BITTERS

Stir and serve in a chilled cocktail coupe. Garnish with a cherry.

THIS IS A clear Negroni variation, with Green Chartreuse—an intensely herbal bittersweet cordial—used in place of Campari. Let's look at how that relates to our archetype.

MANHATTAN		NEGRONI		BIJOU
2 oz. rye (spirit)	→	1 oz. gin (spirit)	→	1 oz. gin (spirit)
1 oz. sweet vermouth (sweet, bitter)	→	1 oz. sweet vermouth (sweet, bitter)	→	1 oz. sweet vermouth (sweet, bitter)
		1 oz. Campari (sweet, bitter)	→	1 oz. Green Chartreuse (sweet, bitter)
				Orange bitters (bitter, complexity)

Tasting notes: Green Chartreuse is really the star of the show here, and with its ABV of 55 percent, the resulting cocktail is deceptively strong. Green Chartreuse is made with 130 botanicals and is one of the more herbal and bitter bottles found behind the bar. Those green, herbal flavors play nicely in general with gin, and the sweet vermouth lengthens the cocktail and makes it rich and round on the palate.

Bonsoni

Stirred classic

1 OZ. FERNET BRANCA
1 OZ. COCCHI VERMOUTH DI TORINO SWEET VERMOUTH
1 OZ. COCCHI AMERICANO
⅛ OZ. ELISIR NOVASALUS

Stir and serve in a chilled cocktail coupe. Garnish with an orange twist.

This is a further variation on the Negroni where the spirit portion is replaced by a bittersweet cordial, Fernet Branca (which weighs in with a respectable ABV of 39 percent). This is definitely a bitter-lover's cocktail, with only vermouth, Cocchi Americano (another A&F wine), a bittersweet cordial, and a scant bar spoon of a bracingly bitter Alpine aperitif, Elisir Novasalus. Things that are really, really bitter have to be balanced by an equal measure of sweetness, so it is no coincidence that all of the ingredients have a considerable amount of sugar too.

Tasting notes: This cocktail is a study in balancing sweet and bitter in a lower ABV cocktail. Fernet and Novasalus are, by themselves, not for the faint of heart, but in this cocktail they are sweetened and balanced by the A&F wines. The orange twist brightens up the deep, dark, bitter flavors in the drink. The Bonsoni is a perfect drink to get your appetite going predinner or to punctuate a giant holiday meal.

MANHATTAN		NEGRONI		BONSONI
2 oz. rye (spirit)	→	1 oz. gin (spirit)	→	1 oz. Fernet Branca (spirit, sweet, bitter)
1 oz. sweet vermouth (sweet, bitter)	→	1 oz. sweet vermouth (sweet, bitter)	→	1 oz. sweet vermouth (sweet, bitter)
		1 oz. Campari (sweet, bitter)	→	1 oz. Cocchi Americano (sweet, bitter)
				⅛ oz. Elisir Novasalus (bitter, complexity)

Old Fashioned

Built classic

1¾ OZ. MAKER'S MARK BOURBON
½ OZ. SIMPLE SYRUP
2 DASHES ANGOSTURA BITTERS
6 DROPS MICAH'S CHERRY SASSAFRAS BITTERS
(SEE APPENDIX)
ORANGE TWIST

Bruise the twist face-down in a tumbler. Add ingredients, then ice, and stir for ten seconds.

IMAGINE THAT IT'S 1806. You've just scored a block of lake ice from the Tudor Ice Company. You cleave a crystal clear chunk and drop it into your bittered sling of whiskey, sugar, water, and bitters. You give it a stir, and you're elated. Two hundred years pass, and the technique and hopefully the outcome are still the same. Lots of bartenders still make the cocktail this way and refer to the Old Fashioned as a "built" cocktail; that is, you build it directly in the glass. You could stir the drink in a shaker with ice and then strain it out over a big cube, but the tradition of building it in the glass generally wins out. Despite not being executed as strictly a stirred cocktail, it resembles our stirred archetype in foiling whiskey with sugar and bitter. Note that we use simple syrup instead of sugar cubes. My experience has been that sugar cubes frequently don't become fully dissolved in a cocktail, leaving our sweet component less than fully represented and our cocktail off balance. Using simple syrup ensures that the exact amount of sugar we need goes directly into our cocktail solution.

2 oz. rye (spirit)	→	1¾ oz. bourbon (spirit)
1 oz. sweet vermouth (sweet, bitter)	→	½ oz. simple syrup (sweet) Angostura bitters Cherry sassafras bitters (bitter, complexity)

TASTING NOTES: The Old Fashioned is the original "cocktail." When made with a smart balance of spirit, sugar, and bitter, it tastes not unlike a well-made Sazerac: perfectly bitter-balanced booze candy. Whiskey and orange essence are a classic combo, and the orange peel plus cherry bitters work well to replace the clunky flavor and aesthetics of mashed up cherries and orange wedges. There's a reason this cocktail exists today much as it did over two hundred years ago. It's damn near perfect.

Orange Artichoke

Stirred original

2 OZ. MAKER'S MARK BOURBON
½ OZ. CARPANO ANTICA SWEET VERMOUTH
½ OZ. AMARO NONINO
½ OZ. CYNAR
2 DASHES ANGOSTURA ORANGE BITTERS

Stir and serve in a tumbler with a single large ice cube. Garnish with an orange twist.

I was teaching my second cocktail class, discussing theory and the Mr. Potato Head method of creating cocktails, and with very little thought reasoned to this cocktail. Sadly, it is more delicious than things I have wrought with much greater intellectual effort. But alas, successful creations start with a sound theoretical approach! This cocktail is a bourbon Manhattan, with the sweet vermouth portion split into three parts.

2 oz. rye (spirit)	→	2 oz. bourbon (spirit)
1 oz. sweet vermouth (sweet, bitter)	→	½ oz. sweet vermouth ½ oz. Amaro Nonino ½ oz. Cynar (sweet, bitter)
		Orange bitters (bitter, complexity)

TASTING NOTES: Cynar is an artichoke-flavored aperitif that is intensely bitter, and at 17 percent ABV, it's a great candidate for using in place of or in conjunction with sweet vermouth. With Cynar being a tad more bitter than sweet vermouth, the cocktail can handle a little bump in sugar. The ½ oz. of Amaro Nonino—an Italian bitter orange cordial—provides just that. Bourbon and orange is a classic combo, and the Cynar–sweet vermouth–Amaro Nonino combo serves to sufficiently sweeten and bitter this cocktail. Orange bitters and an orange twist bring additional flavor and brightness.

Dead Rosetti

Stirred original

2 OZ. BUFFALO TRACE BOURBON
¾ OZ. MICAH'S CRANBERRY CORDIAL (SEE APPENDIX)
½ OZ. CAMPARI
8 DROPS MICAH'S ORANGE SPICE BITTERS (SEE APPENDIX)

Stir and serve in a tumbler with a single large ice cube. Garnish with an orange twist.

One of my favorite TV shows is *Boardwalk Empire*. Season 3 was particularly good, due in part to a wild, donkey-of-a-man antagonist named Gyp Rosetti. He was a bitterly mean Italian guy who made a living by stealing whiskey and killing lots of people. It seemed only natural to pay a little tribute to ol' Gyp with a Manhattan riff featuring bourbon whiskey and the notorious Italian bittersweet cordial Campari.

2 oz. rye (spirit)	→	2 oz. bourbon (spirit)
1 oz. sweet vermouth (sweet, bitter)	→	½ oz. Campari (sweet, bitter) ¾ oz. cranberry cordial (sweet)
		Orange spice bitters (bitter, complexity)

TASTING NOTES: For my palate, Campari is rarely able to sufficiently sweeten a cocktail on its own. The cranberry cordial is there to shore up the sweetness, as well as adding complementary mulled cranberry flavors. The orange spice bitters and cranberry cordial have notes of vanilla, cinnamon, clove, mace, and cardamom that make this cocktail very much a spiced Christmas Manhattan riff. It works out neatly as winter is the best time to get fresh cranberries to make the cordial.

Improved Toronto

Stirred original

2 OZ. RITTENHOUSE RYE
½ OZ. BRANCA MENTA
¼ OZ. FERNET BRANCA
2 DASHES ANGOSTURA BITTERS

Stir and serve in a tumbler with a single large ice cube. Garnish with a lemon twist.

This is a minimalist riff on the Toronto cocktail, a municipally eponymous relative of the Manhattan. The Toronto is simply 2 oz. rye, ¼ oz. Fernet Branca, and ¼ oz. simple syrup with an orange twist. To me, this cocktail is too boozy, and could use just an extra push of both sweet and bitter, and maybe another flavor to fill out the rye. Here's how I reworked it, starting from our archetype.

MANHATTAN		TORONTO		IMPROVED TORONTO
2 oz. rye (spirit)	→	2 oz. rye (spirit)	→	2 oz. rye (spirit)
1 oz. sweet vermouth (sweet, bitter)	→	¼ oz. Fernet Branca (sweet, bitter) ¼ oz. simple syrup (sweet)	→	¼ oz. Fernet Branca ½ oz. Branca Menta (sweet, bitter)
				Angostura bitters (bitter, complexity)

TASTING NOTES: Branca Menta is Fernet's minty, sweeter, nicer cousin. It has resinous mint and eucalyptus notes, and goes well with gin and whiskey. This cocktail is boozy, but the Fernet Branca and Branca Menta sufficiently sweeten and bitter the heavy pour of rye. The Improved Toronto tastes of rich rye, mint, and spice, and the lemon twist brightens and complements these flavors—the mint especially.

Blackfriar Cocktail

Stirred original

1½ OZ. PLYMOUTH SLOE GIN
1 OZ. PLYMOUTH GIN
½ OZ. BYRRH
¼ OZ. FERNET BRANCA

Stir and serve in a chilled cocktail coupe. Garnish with a lemon twist.

As someone who has long thought the taste of alcohol was aggressive and unpalatable, some of the first drinks I ever choked down are embarrassing to mention. But here goes: in the year 2000, nothing—nothing, mind you—was more my jam than a Sloe Gin Fizz. And a sugary, crappy one made with $7 Mr. Boston's sloe gin and bottled sour mix. I was such a child . . . but childhood serves as inspiration in adulthood! This is a Sloe Gin Fizz all grown up, after having gone to grad school, having purchased a house, and finally as an adult having embraced stirred cocktails. This derivation is not entirely straightforward, as I had to amp up the amount of sloe gin—Plymouth sloe gin that actually tastes of sloe or blackthorn berries—to an amount that doesn't exactly map onto simple proportions. The sloe gin provides a notable amount of sweetness and also weighs in at 26 percent ABV, and 1½ oz. of it does contribute to our spirit base.

2 oz. rye (spirit)	→	1 oz. gin (spirit)
	→	1½ oz. sloe gin (spirit, sweet)
1 oz. sweet vermouth (sweet, bitter)	→	
	→	½ oz. Byrrh ¼ oz. Fernet Branca (sweet, bitter)

Tasting notes: Byrrh quinquina is an A&F wine that is made with a red wine base and bittered with cinchona, with raspberry notes that complement the sloe gin. The ¼ oz. of Fernet is there to ensure we have enough bitterness to balance out the sweet in the Byrrh and sloe gin. The 1 oz. of Plymouth gin is there to reinforce the alcohol backbone of the cocktail. The lemon twist brightens up the bitters and berries. Hopefully, this cocktail redeems the poor taste of my adolescence.

Montmartre

Stirred original

1 OZ. HAYMAN'S OLD TOM GIN
1 OZ. CONTRATTO BIANCO VERMOUTH
1 OZ. YELLOW CHARTREUSE
2 DASHES ANGOSTURA ORANGE BITTERS

Stir and serve in a chilled cocktail coupe. Garnish with a lemon twist.

This cocktail is simply a white Bijou, which we identified earlier as a Negroni variant. We sub a bianco or white vermouth for sweet vermouth, and Yellow Chartreuse for Green Chartreuse.

MANHATTAN		NEGRONI		MONTMARTRE
2 oz. rye (spirit)	→	1 oz. gin (spirit)	→	1 oz. gin (spirit)
1 oz. sweet vermouth (sweet, bitter)	→	1 oz. sweet vermouth (sweet, bitter)	→	1 oz. Contratto Bianco (sweet, bitter)
		1 oz. Campari (sweet, bitter)	→	1 oz. Yellow Chartreuse (sweet, bitter)
				Orange bitters (bitter, complexity)

Tasting notes: This is a lighter but still rich version of the Bijou. The Contratto Bianco has white-raisin depth and bitter sweetness, and the Yellow Chartreuse contributes notes of honey and bitter herbs. To me, this cocktail tastes like bright flowers, white raisins, honey, and herbs in a glass.

Mean Old Man

Stirred original

1 OZ. LAPHROAIG 10-YEAR SINGLE MALT SCOTCH WHISKY
1 OZ. CAMPARI
½ OZ. CARPANO ANTICA SWEET VERMOUTH
½ OZ. ZUCCA

Stir and serve in a chilled cocktail coupe. Garnish with an orange twist.

Zucca is still something that makes me gag. It's a rhubarb amaro (a bittersweet cordial from Italy, if you recall from chapter 1), and it has notes of burnt meat and ripe cheese on the nose. When I first got it, I let it sit on the shelf for a year, uncertain what to do with it. After the bottle had gathered some dust, a patron challenged me to make him an aggressively, offensively bitter and smoky cocktail. I thought of the things I liked least—iodiney scotch and stinky, stinky Zucca—and plugged them into a Negroni recipe. It worked! Scotch lovers love this drink, and I have to say that I don't think it's terrible. It is balanced! The stink of both the scotch and the Zucca are placed in the balanced frame of a classic and it simply works. This is another example of how knowing a successful scaffold can help you transform aggressive ingredients with little effort. In this drink the 1 oz. of sweet vermouth is split into two equal potions: ½ oz. Zucca and ½ oz. sweet vermouth.

MANHAT-TAN		NEGRONI		MEAN OLD MAN
2 oz. rye (spirit)	→	1 oz. gin (spirit)	→	1 oz. scotch (spirit)
1 oz. sweet vermouth (sweet, bitter)	→	1 oz. sweet vermouth (sweet, bitter)	→	½ oz. sweet vermouth ½ oz. Zucca (sweet, bitter)
		1 oz. Campari (sweet, bitter)	→	1 oz. Campari (sweet, bitter)

Tasting notes: The ½ oz. of sweet vermouth is the yummy part of this drink. It adds enough vanilla and caramel depth for the aggressive flavors of smoke and bitter to play nicely in the foreground. Given the ingredients, the drink is surprisingly full, with grain, smoke, and bittersweetness mingling harmoniously with a bright top note of orange peel.

Talking Serpent

Stirred original

1 OZ. JOHNNY WALKER BLACK BLENDED SCOTCH WHISKY
1 OZ. PUNT E MES SWEET VERMOUTH
½ OZ. CIDER REDUCTION (SEE APPENDIX)
¼ OZ. ST. ELIZABETH ALLSPICE DRAM

Stir and serve in a tumbler with a single large ice cube. Garnish with an orange twist.

I try to challenge myself to make scotch cocktails because, in general, scotch is not my favorite. I think scotch is a good candidate for stirred cocktails because its barley (and frequent peat and smoke) presence is unmistakable and can stand shoulder to shoulder with big, bitter flavors without being overwhelmed. Smokey Johnny Walker Black and apple immediately reminds me of the Fall of Adam in the book of Genesis (in the Bible, if you remember from Sunday school), so the Talking Serpent is a nod to my roots! This cocktail is essentially a scotch cider Manhattan, but the proportions look more Negroni-esque. Let's open the hood and take a peek.

Tasting notes: Punt e Mes ties the Scotch and cider together with deep, raisiny, dark fruit notes. Allspice dram, an intensely allspice-flavored bittersweet cordial, is a great baking-spice accent to the cider, the whisky, and the vermouth. This cocktail comes out tasting like a bittersweet and seductive kiss from the Devil himself.

MANHATTAN		NEGRONI		TALKING SERPENT
2 oz. rye (spirit)	→	1 oz. gin (spirit)	→	1 oz. scotch (spirit)
1 oz. sweet vermouth (sweet, bitter)	→	1 oz. sweet vermouth (sweet, bitter)	→	1 oz. sweet vermouth (sweet, bitter)
		1 oz. Campari (sweet, bitter)	→	¼ oz. allspice dram (sweet, bitter) ½ oz. cider reduction (sweet)

Lord of the Flies

Stirred original

1 OZ. TANQUERAY GIN
1 OZ. CAPPELLETTI APERITIVO
1 OZ. RANSIO SEC

Stir and serve in a chilled cocktail coupe. Garnish with an orange twist.

Cappelletti, Campari, and Aperol are a trio of famously red aperitifs from Italy. What is less known is that at one point all three took their pigment from a dye called carmine, found in the wings of a single insect, *Dactylopius coccus.* Cappelletti is the only one that still uses this natural dye, and its flavor is a bit softer than Campari, with less bitter, more sugar, and a rich wine base complemented by bitter orange and vanilla notes. Ransio Sec is a fun "wine" I was introduced to by a local wine and cocktail enthusiast in here in Charlottesville. Essentially it's wine that is left out in the sun to fully oxidize, imparting some strangely delicious flavors. The wine ends up somewhere between a bone dry sherry and a madeira, with tart but rich notes of nuts and mushrooms. When paired with a rich aperitif, it can function like sweet vermouth in a cocktail … so we have another Negroni variation!

MANHATTAN		NEGRONI		LORD OF THE FLIES
2 oz. rye (spirit)	→	1 oz. gin (spirit)	→	1 oz. gin (spirit)
1 oz. sweet vermouth (sweet, bitter)	→	1 oz. sweet vermouth (sweet, bitter)	→	1 oz. Ransio Sec (sweet, bitter)
		1 oz. Campari (sweet, bitter)	→	1 oz. Cappelletti (sweet, bitter)

TASTING NOTES: The deep wisdom of the Negroni never ceases to amaze me. Here is another example. Cappelletti really fills out the dryness of the Ransio Sec and gin. The tartness of Ransio Sec with the bitterness of Cappelletti are complemented by the heavy juniper in Tanqueray, and the orange ties the bow on a cocktail of spice, nuts, wine, and bitter herbs. Ransio Sec, while increasing in popularity, may be hard to find. An oloroso sherry or dry madeira would work in its place in a pinch.

Greater Antilles

Stirred original

¾ OZ. APPLETON'S 12-YEAR RUM
¾ OZ. PIERRE FERRAND DRY CURAÇAO
¾ OZ. COCCHI VERMOUTH DI TORINO SWEET VERMOUTH
½ OZ. PEDRO XIMÉNEZ SHERRY
2 DASHES ANGOSTURA BITTERS
ABSINTHE RINSE

Stir and serve in a tumbler with an absinthe rinse and a single large ice cube. Garnish with an orange twist.

If you hadn't noticed by now, I like my stirred cocktails richly flavored. I like vanilla, nuts, orange zest, and baking spices. I'm hip to that criticism of myself, but alas I must follow the pull of my juvenile palate! Here is another riff on those flavors I reach for, inspired by the proportions of the Vieux Carré. This cocktail is a bit sweeter than a Vieux Carré, as I replace ¾ oz. of spirit with ¾ oz. of dry curaçao, a cognac-based orange liqueur that weighs in with a respectable 40 percent ABV.

Tasting notes: You may have noticed that we added additional sugar to our Vieux Carré skeleton. One trick for cocktails that are bordering on being too sweet is to add a couple dashes of bitters, or just a bar spoon or rinse of a bittersweet cordial. I do both here. Absinthe and orange is a classic combination, and just a rinse of the tumbler with absinthe adds an extra dimension of flavor and balances our sugar with bitterness. This cocktail tastes like my aforementioned weakness for things that are richly rummy, nutty, and spiced, presented in the boozy framework of a successful, classic cocktail.

MANHATTAN		VIEUX CARRÉ		GREATER ANTILLES
2 oz. rye (spirit)	→	¾ oz. rye (spirit)	→	¾ oz. rum (spirit)
		¾ oz. cognac (spirit)	→	¾ oz. dry curaçao (spirit, sweet)
1 oz. sweet vermouth (sweet, bitter)	→	¾ oz. sweet vermouth (sweet, bitter)	→	¾ oz. sweet vermouth (sweet, bitter)
		¼ oz. Bénédictine (sweet, bitter)	→	½ oz. sherry (sweet) Absinthe rinse Angostura bitters (bitter, complexity)

Nelson County Gentleman

Carbonated and shaken original

2 OZ. RITTENHOUSE RYE
¾ OZ. BIRCH SYRUP (SEE APPENDIX)
¼ OZ. ROOT
6 DROPS BOB'S PEPPERMINT BITTERS

Combine ingredients in a cocktail carbonator and charge with CO_2. Shake (!) for 12 seconds. Vent the carbonator slowly. Gently pour carbonated cocktail into a tumbler with ice. Garnish with an orange twist.

I've included this drink with the stirred cocktails because it shows how the qualitative aspects (and flavors) of a cocktail can be radically transformed by the technique employed to mix it—in this case, carbonating and shaking a cocktail you might expect to be stirred. I stumbled onto this cocktail when I was working on a Virginia terroir Manhattan with some local birch and sassafras. I then discovered Root, an intensely bittersweet cordial with American root beer botanicals, and thought it might be a good fit for the idea. Attempts to make a rye-birch-Root Manhattan were solidly OK, but just for the hell of it, I put the cocktail in our cocktail carbonator. The extra dilution, aeration, and carbonation made the drink read like a boozy root beer, not a silky smooth Manhattan riff. It's been a hit at the restaurant. Not a half-bad name, either. Let's see how it relates to a Manhattan.

2 oz. rye (spirit)	→	2 oz. rye (spirit)
1 oz. sweet vermouth (sweet, bitter)	→	¼ oz. Root (sweet, bitter) ¾ oz. birch syrup (sweet)
		Bob's peppermint bitters (bitter, complexity)

At home, in the absence of a Soda Stream or fancy cocktail carbonator, you could rework this as a stirred cocktail. Just remember the loss of carbonation means a loss of acidity, so you may want to adjust your other components just a bit. Also, good maple syrup works in place of birch in a pinch.

TASTING NOTES: In researching root beer, I was interested to learn that wintergreen and spearmint are the dominant but forgotten flavors in the brew. The peppermint bitters are there to accent these flavors in the Root bittersweet cordial. This cocktail is a boozy, fizzy, bitter-balanced soda that weaves together rye, birch, peppermint, and spice. Interestingly enough, some of the CO_2 added by the carbonator goes into solution as carbonic acid ($H_2O + CO_2 = H_2CO_3$), a weak acid that does change the pH of the cocktail and pings the buds on your palate that detect sour. Consequently, we have both bitterness and acidity to balance the ¾ oz. of birch syrup.

Daiquiri

Shaken cocktail archetype

2 OZ. PUSSER'S BRITISH NAVY RUM
½ OZ. SIMPLE SYRUP
½ OZ. LIME JUICE

Shake and double strain (see chapter 2) into a chilled cocktail coupe. Garnish with a lime wheel.

THE DAIQUIRI—THE CARIBBEAN concoction of rum, lime, and sugar—likely existed under a different name centuries before. After all, it is just punch stripped of the fussier elements of tea and spice, right? The Daiquiri represents the bare minimum that is required of a successful shaken cocktail: spirit, sugar, and citrus. I'm sure you know the drill by know, but let's classify our ingredients so we can better manipulate them:

2 oz. rum	Spirit
½ oz. simple syrup	Sweet
½ oz. lime	Sour

The skeleton of our Daiquiri can be found in most classic and contemporary shaken cocktails: about 2 oz. spirit, about ½ oz. lemon or lime juice, and about ½ oz. simple syrup or some equivalent. Again, *nearly all shaken cocktails have an approximation of this formula at their core.* This is where you want to start when crafting your own shaken cocktails.

TASTING NOTES: Lots of folks like to use light rum in a Daiquiri, but I like the extra flavor that comes with an aged rum. To me, aged rum tastes a bit more like molasses, and many have toasted marshmallow and faint licorice notes on the palate. Given my love of cake and things that taste of vanilla and spice, I like aged rum. A Pusser's Daiquiri has this toasted marshmallow nuttiness, sweetened with sugar, and brightened and balanced with lime. I serve this with a lime wheel and not a wedge because with these particular ratios, I find it to be balanced and not in need of any additional acidity. Also, to me a perfectly cut wheel is just darn sexy floating in a fancy coupe.

Bee's Knees

Shaken classic

2 OZ. TANQUERAY GIN
¾ OZ. HONEY SYRUP
¾ OZ. LEMON JUICE
3 DASHES MICAH'S LAVENDER BITTERS (SEE APPENDIX)

Shake and double strain into a chilled cocktail coupe. Garnish with a lemon twist.

Spirit, sugar, citrus. This is the essence of shaken classic cocktails. In this classic, gin subs for rum, lemon for lime, and honey syrup for simple syrup. If you remember from chapter 1, you make honey syrup with one part hot water and one part honey.

2 oz. rum (spirit)	→	2 oz. gin (spirit)
½ oz. simple syrup (sweet)	→	¾ oz. honey syrup (sweet)
½ oz. lime juice (sour)	→	¾ oz. lemon juice (sour)
		Lavender bitters (bitter, complexity)

Tasting notes: This cocktail is perfect for spring: floral gin, sweetened with honey and balanced with lemon. I add just a few dashes of lavender bitters for complexity and to echo the time of year.

Being a bit obsessed with things that smell nice, I have a garden full of herbs—lavender in particular. It's easy to make a tincture with the flowers, or if you're feeling ambitious, a full-on lavender bitters.

Lion's Tail

Shaken classic

1¾ OZ. ELIJAH CRAIG 12-YEAR BOURBON
½ OZ. ST. ELIZABETH ALLSPICE DRAM
½ OZ. LIME JUICE
¼ OZ. SIMPLE SYRUP
2 DASHES ANGOSTURA BITTERS

Shake and double strain into a chilled cocktail coupe. Garnish with a lime twist.

This is one of the few shaken bourbon classics. It's just a reworked Daiquiri with bourbon and allspice. Because the allspice dram is potent and bitter, we need to keep a little simple syrup in the recipe to balance the bitterness and spice in the cocktail.

2 oz. rum (spirit)	→	1¾ oz. bourbon (spirit)
½ oz. simple syrup (sweet)	→	¼ oz. simple syrup (sweet) ½ oz. allspice dram (sweet, bitter)
½ oz. lime juice (sour)	→	½ oz. lime juice (sour)
		Angostura bitters (bitter, complexity)

TASTING NOTES: Bourbon and spice is what this cocktail is all about, and the oaky Elijah Craig is a good pick for pairing with allspice dram. Lime stands up to the allspice just a bit more than lemon would, and this is one of the few times you'll see lime with bourbon in a classic. Angostura bitters fills out the spice on the palate with a little clove and cinnamon.

Whiskey Sour

Shaken classic

2 OZ. BUFFALO TRACE BOURBON
¾ OZ. SIMPLE SYRUP
¾ OZ. LEMON JUICE
½ OZ. EGG WHITE

Dry shake (see chapter 2), then shake with ice. Double strain into a chilled cocktail coupe. Garnish with a bitters swirl (see chapter 2) and an orange and cherry flag.

How times have changed: when I first started bartending and someone asked for a sour, I reached for canned sour mix and a splash of soda. Good for volume and young palates, bad for making things yummy. Fortunately, *sour* has reclaimed some of its historical semantic domain in the world of cocktails—meaning a twice-shaken cocktail with spirit, sweet, sour, and egg white. The Whiskey Sour is just that, and if you compare it to our archetype, it looks a lot like a Daiquiri but with bourbon and a little egg white.

2 oz. rum (spirit)	→	2 oz. bourbon (spirit)
½ oz. simple syrup (sweet)	→	¾ oz. simple syrup (sweet)
½ oz. lime juice (sour)	→	¾ oz. lemon juice (sour)
		½ oz. egg white (length, mouth feel)

Tasting notes: Learn this scaffold! It is the key to executing balanced shaken cocktails with egg whites. We'll return to this formula and riff on it over and over. Sugar and lemon bring out bourbon's caramel corn notes, and the egg white softens the whiskey tannins and makes the drink light on the palate. And remember from chapter 2 that egg-white cocktails need to be shaken first *without* ice and then shaken for twelve seconds *with* ice to get the proper degree of emulsification, aeration, chilling, and dilution.

Clover Club

Shaken classic

2 OZ. GREENALL'S GIN
1 OZ. RASPBERRY CORDIAL (SEE APPENDIX)
½ OZ. LEMON JUICE
½ OZ. EGG WHITE

Dry shake, then shake with ice. Double strain into a chilled cocktail coupe. Garnish with Campari sprinkles (see appendix).

Daiquiri, sub gin for rum and add egg white. Lemon subs for lime. Replace the simple syrup with raspberry cordial, and with just a few substitutions we've Mr.-Potato-Headed our way to yet another classic cocktail.

2 oz. rum (spirit)	→	2 oz. gin (spirit)
½ oz. simple syrup (sweet)	→	1 oz. raspberry cordial (sweet)
½ oz. lime juice (sour)	→	½ oz. lemon juice (sour)
		½ oz. egg white (length, mouth feel)

Tasting notes: Ever stick your nose in a carton of fresh raspberries? When they're ripe, they're fragrant almost to the point of seeming artificial—for me evocative of the rare blue raspberry

Slurpees of my youth. Fragrant berries and fragrant gin, sweetened with sugar, balanced with lemon, and lightened on the palate with egg white. So many things in adulthood are much better versions of things from youth . . . and with Campari sprinkles no less! The sprinkles, in addition to being fun and aesthetically pleasing, add a sporadic crunch and pleasant bitter note that balances the raspberry sweetness in the cocktail.

Sidecar

Shaken classic

1½ OZ. COURVOISIER VS COGNAC
¾ OZ. PIERRE FERRAND DRY CURAÇAO
¾ OZ. LEMON JUICE
¼ OZ. SIMPLE SYRUP

Shake and double strain into a coupe with a half-sugared rim. Garnish with an orange half-wheel.

THIS WAS ONE of the first classics I discovered as a young man that I really liked. To me this cocktail tasted like an orange brandy sour, with a sugar rim no less to please my kiddy taste buds. I'm sure that version was made with bottled sour mix, and sadly it did not trigger a eureka moment that wouldn't come until years later. Equipped as an adult with the Daiquiri recipe as my guide, I reasoned to the Sidecar as follows.

2 oz. rum (spirit)	→	1½ oz. cognac (spirit)
	→	¾ oz. dry curaçao (spirit, sweet)
½ oz. simple syrup (sweet)	→	
	→	¼ oz. simple syrup (sweet)
½ oz. lime juice (sour)	→	¾ oz. lemon juice (sour)

TASTING NOTES: We dialed down the cognac quantity because it is augmented by dry curaçao, an orange liqueur that's 40 percent ABV. Dry curaçao contributes both sweetness and significant alcohol content, and we balance that with a healthy ¾ oz. of lemon juice and just a pinch more simple syrup to check the extra ¼ oz. of booze. This cocktail is very much an orange brandy sour for adults: structured with cognac, sweetened (and further fortified) with dry curaçao, and balanced with lemon.

Margarita

Shaken classic

> 2 OZ. HERRADURA SILVER TEQUILA
> ¾ OZ. COINTREAU
> ¾ OZ. LIME JUICE
> ½ OZ. SIMPLE SYRUP

Shake and double strain into a coupe with a half-salted rim. Garnish with a lime wheel.

Like the Daiquiri, the Margarita has gotten a bad rap. Both have been abused with bottled sour mix and blenders, but when made properly both are pure expressions of their respective spirits in a shaken cocktail medium. There are a million ways to make a basic margarita—with simple syrup and no orange liqueur, with agave syrup as the sole sweetener, with aged tequila instead of silver, and more—but I like using a silver tequila with just a bit of orange in the mix via orange liqueur. Since we are adding additional booze with ¾ oz. of Cointreau (40 percent ABV), we'll need a robust amount of our sour component, and also a tad more sweetness.

Tasting notes: Silver tequila is a fascinating distillate. It's one of the few nonneutral distillates where the unaged version has flavors that are rich and pleasant. I get notes of roasted pineapple and cucumber with nicer silver tequilas, and these flavors are perfect with lime and sugar. This Margarita is silver tequila filled out with lime and sugar, and complemented by a hit of orange from Cointreau.

2 oz. rum (spirit)	→	2 oz. tequila (spirit)
	→	¾ oz. Cointreau (spirit, sweet)
½ oz. simple syrup (sweet)	→	
	→	½ oz. simple syrup (sweet)
½ oz. lime juice (sour)	→	¾ oz. lime juice (sour)

137 • *Stirred & Shaken Cocktails*

French 75

Shaken classic

1 OZ. COURVOISIER VS COGNAC
½ OZ. LEMON JUICE
½ OZ. SIMPLE SYRUP
2 OZ. CHAMPAGNE OR OTHER DRY SPARKLING WINE

Shake all ingredients except champagne. Double strain into a chilled cocktail coupe and top with champagne. Garnish with a lemon twist.

The French 75 is a glass of champagne on steroids: wine fortified by a wine distillate. But at its core, there's a shaken cocktail that resembles a Daiquiri, with the spirit dialed down just a bit so as not to overwhelm the wine.

2 oz. rum (spirit)	→	1 oz. cognac (spirit)
½ oz. simple syrup (sweet)	→	½ oz. simple syrup (sweet)
½ oz. lime juice (sour)	→	½ oz. lemon juice (sour)
		2 oz. champagne (length, flavor)

When making this cocktail (and others like it with carbonated ingredients), remember not to put the fizzy stuff in the shaker, or your bubbles will be flat in the final drink.

TASTING NOTES: The French 75 can be made with either gin or cognac. I like to use cognac because I think the barrel flavors add some rich notes that complement the yeasty sparkling wine. This also is the first time we've encountered a significant quantity of a lengthener in a classic.

Not surprisingly another variation of the French 75 exists: the Airmail, with rum subbing for cognac, lime for lemon, and honey syrup for simple syrup. Both beverages read more like balanced, fortified sparkling wines than Daiquiri variants, and such is the genius of the lengthener. Lengtheners bring auxiliary flavors to the forefront of a beverage and can help you be prolifically creative with little effort.

Gimlet

Shaken classic

2 OZ. BARR HILL GIN
1 OZ. LIME CORDIAL (SEE APPENDIX)

Shake and double strain into a chilled cocktail coupe with a half-sugared rim. Garnish with a lime wheel.

This is a minimally reworked Daiquri with gin. Gin and lime get along famously in this cocktail, and we use a lime cordial that incorporates both our sweet and sour components in one ingredient. Lime cordial is preferred over a combo of lime juice and sugar, as the cordial is made with lime zest or oil, and is consequently more intensely limey and bright.

2 oz. rum (spirit)	→	2 oz. gin (spirit)
½ oz. simple syrup (sweet)	→	1 oz. lime cordial (sweet, sour)
½ oz. lime juice (sour)	→	

Tasting notes: Barr Hill gin is incredibly junipery, to the point of smelling like a forest full of evergreens. This greenness goes perfectly with our bright cordial made with fresh lime juice, lime zest, and sugar. This versatile cocktail captures the evergreen essence of Christmastime, as well as being a cold and tart foil to the heat of a summer day.

Corpse Reviver No. 2

Shaken classic

---

1 OZ. BEEFEATER GIN
1 OZ. COINTREAU
1 OZ. LILLET BLANC
½ OZ. LEMON JUICE
ABSINTHE RINSE

Shake and double strain into a chilled cocktail coupe with an absinthe rinse. Garnish with a lemon twist.

THIS COCKTAIL IS in a class of drinks called pick-me-ups: exceedingly drinkable *and* strong, a perfect shot in the arm in the morning after having over-imbibed the night before. It *is* a riff on a Daiquiri, but it's notable as it's one of the first shaken classics to introduce a hefty ounce of an A&F wine into our Daiquiri skeleton. We also split our spirit portion with gin and Cointreau, both weighing in at around 40 percent ABV, to form the alcohol backbone of the drink. It's almost Negroni-esque if you look at the 1:1:1 ratio . . . patterns, patterns, patterns.

TASTING NOTES: The Corpse Reviver No. 2 is a no-brainer classic: the flavors of lemon and orange, paired with absinthe, structured with gin, and lengthened with Lillet Blanc. It's always been a little shocking to me that even though the only nonalcoholic ingredient in this cocktail is lemon, it drinks like a brunch cocktail. It's a study in balancing spirit, sweet, sour, *and* bitter. The Corpse Reviver No. 2 is a great scaffold for creating cocktails that pair equal parts spirit, cordial, and A&F wine with citrus.

2 oz. rum (spirit)	→	1 oz. gin (spirit)
	→	1 oz. Cointreau (spirit, sweet)
½ oz. simple syrup (sweet)	→	
	→	1 oz. Lillet Blanc (length, sweet, bitter, complexity)
½ oz. lime juice (sour)	→	½ oz. lemon juice (sour)
		Absinthe (bitter, complexity)

Punch

Classic cocktail diluted with tea

OLEO SACCHARUM, MADE WITH
- 5 CUPS SUGAR
- PEELS OF 30 LEMONS

JUICE FROM 30 LEMONS, ABOUT 4 CUPS

TEA, MADE WITH
- ¾ CUP LOOSE BLACK TEA LEAVES
- 5 QUARTS WATER

1500 ML. AGED RUM

First, make the oleo saccharum. Peel lemons, trying to get as little pith as possible. Take the peels and stir them with sugar, allowing them to sit for at least an hour or until the oils in the lemons start to dissolve the sugar into an oily syrup.

While sugar macerates on lemon peels, bring water to a boil. Once at a boil, remove from heat and steep loose tea for 10 minutes. If you steep the tea for much longer than 15 minutes, your punch will be unpleasantly astringent from the over-extracted tea.

Allow tea to cool, and pour cooled tea over oleo saccharum to dissolve any remaining sugar. Strain the peels from the tea and oleo mixture, and combine the mixture with rum and lemon juice. Adjust spirit, sugar, and citrus to taste, bearing in mind that a room-temperature punch will be a little sweeter on the palate than a cold punch.

Refrigerate and serve the punch cold. Serve with a grate of fresh nutmeg and a wheel of lemon or lime. Makes approximately 2½ gallons.

Tasting notes: This is a super fancy Daiquiri! It's a rum-citrus-sugar combo with dilution coming from tea instead of from shaking. Rum provides the body of the drink, the oleo fills out and sweetens the rum, the lemon balances the sugared booze, and the tea adds length, complexity, and a pleasant note of tannin bitterness. Like the Daiquiri, there are a million ways to riff on punch: vary the tea, use a different combination of spirits (rum with brandy, rum with gin, brandy with whiskey, and rum with bourbon are all classic combos), substitute fresh fruit for a cup or more of the sugar in the recipe, and so on.

Smokey Dokey

Shaken original

2 OZ. DEL MAGUEY VIDA MEZCAL
½ OZ. LILLET BLANC
½ OZ. LIME JUICE
1 TBSP. ORANGE CONFIT (SEE APPENDIX)
8 DROPS HABANERO TINCTURE (SEE APPENDIX)

Shake and double strain into a chilled cocktail coupe. Garnish with an orange half-wheel.

MEZCAL, IF YOU remember from chapter 1, is an aggressively earthy and smoky distillate from Central America. Plugging it directly into a Daiquiri recipe will yield an assertively smoky cocktail so we definitely need some other assertive flavors to balance that smoke. In the Smokey Dokey, I added a healthy tablespoon of orange confit (essentially a marmalade made with orange peels, juice, and sugar) in place of simple syrup, a hint of habanero, and just a little length and complexity via Lillet Blanc, an A&F wine.

2 oz. rum (spirit)	→	2 oz. mezcal (spirit)
½ oz. simple syrup (sweet)	→	1 tbsp. orange confit (sweet)
½ oz. lime juice (sour)	→	½ oz. lime juice (sour)
		½ oz. Lillet Blanc (length, sweet, bitter, complexity) Habanero (complexity)

TASTING NOTES: The Smokey Dokey nicely tames the smoke of mezcal by pairing it with intense orange and habanero flavors. The Lillet Blanc adds complexity and length, and lime provides the necessary sour ingredient to balance the booze and sugar. I generally like to pair mezcal with bold flavors to keep the smoke in check.

Bourbon Peach Sour

Shaken original

2 OZ. W. L. WELLER RESERVE BOURBON
¼ CUP MACERATED PEACHES (SEE APPENDIX)
½ OZ. LEMON JUICE
½ OZ. EGG WHITE

Muddle peaches in shaker (see chapter 2). Dry shake, then shake with ice. Double strain into a chilled cocktail coupe. Garnish with a bitters swirl.

The more I make drinks the more I'm convinced that simplicity is an exceedingly valid way to approach good ingredients. Bourbon and peaches (especially when the peaches are ripe and in season) are a match made in heaven, and getting them harmoniously integrated in a cocktail is only a matter of making sure our other requisite ingredients—sweet and sour/bitter—are represented unobtrusively, in this case via lemon and sugar. The egg whites are there to help emulsify our macerated, muddled, and then shaken peaches. Remember from chapter 2 that egg whites are perfect when you have something particulate that you need to emulsify in your cocktail.

Tasting notes: Here in the mountains of Virginia we have a good number of apple and peach orchards, and there is really nothing better than fresh peaches at the end of June. They are mood-enhancingly fragrant, juicy, and delicious. When they are super ripe, I dial back my macerating ratio to 2 cups fruit to ¾ cup sugar and omit the wine, as the peaches suck up and dissolve all of the sugar. This cocktail is the essence of peach fortified and structured around the sweet caramel flavor of bourbon. Egg white lengthens the cocktail, softens the bourbon, and emulsifies our perfectly ripe peaches.

2 oz. rum (spirit)	→	2 oz. bourbon (spirit)
½ oz. simple syrup (sweet)	→	¼ cup macerated peaches (sweet)
½ oz. lime juice (sour)	→	½ oz. lemon juice (sour)
		½ oz. egg white (length, mouth feel, emulsification)

Carpetbagger

Shaken original

2 OZ. OLD OVERHOLT RYE
1 OZ. PINEAPPLE CORDIAL (SEE APPENDIX)
½ OZ. LEMON JUICE
¼ OZ. FERNET BRANCA
PINCH MINT LEAVES

Shake and double strain into a chilled cocktail coupe. Garnish with a mint sprig and lemon half-wheel.

THIS IS A Daiquiri riff where we explore adding depth and complexity, as well as a hint of our requisite bitter, via a scant ¼ oz. of a bittersweet cordial, Fernet Branca.

2 oz. rum (spirit)	→	2 oz. rye (spirit)
½ oz. simple syrup (sweet)	→	1 oz. pineapple cordial (sweet)
½ oz. lime juice (sour)	→	½ oz. lemon juice (sour)
		¼ oz. Fernet Branca (sweet, bitter, complexity) Mint (complexity)

TASTING NOTES: Here we have a light, bready rye, sweetened with pineapple cordial, balanced with lemon, and accented by the brightness of fresh mint paired with the bittersweet cordial Fernet Branca. Fernet does wonders to reinforce the mint notes in this drink, as well as adding considerable depth of flavor without too much bitterness. Without it the drink is good, but the addition of Fernet demonstrates how just a sparing ¼ oz. of the right bittersweet accent can elevate existing flavors in a cocktail.

Paw Paw Daiquiri

Shaken original

1 OZ. BACARDI SILVER RUM
¾ OZ. PUSSER'S BRITISH NAVY RUM
1 OZ. PAW PAW CORDIAL (SEE APPENDIX)
½ OZ. LIME JUICE
⅛ OZ. LUXARDO MARASCHINO

Shake and double strain into a chilled cocktail coupe. Garnish with a lime wheel.

When naming drinks, sometimes I like to err on the side of being descriptive and not clever, just to avoid a series of "What's in that again?" conversations over the course of the evening. That and I frequently come up with drink names that are risqué, inside jokes, or alarmingly bad puns. As the name suggests and as the recipe shows, this is a minimally reworked Daiquiri, inspired by the late fall crop of paw paws that we get here in the Blue Ridge Mountains of Virginia. The main changes to our archetype are splitting the spirit base into two kinds of rum and using a different sweet component. We also add a bar spoon of Luxardo maraschino to bring a soapy, fruity, bitter accent to our paw paws.

2 oz. rum (spirit)	→	1 oz. light rum ¾ oz. aged rum (spirit)
½ oz. simple syrup (sweet)	→	1 oz. paw paw cordial (sweet)
½ oz. lime juice (sour)	→	½ oz. lime juice (sour)
		⅛ oz. Luxardo maraschino (bitter, complexity)

TASTING NOTES: What is a paw paw, you ask? Foraging has only recently become hip in fancy restaurants, and I had never seen a wild, foraged paw paw until two years ago. Truth be told, the texture of paw paws is kind of custardy, mushy, and gross, but the flavor is really interesting. They taste like a cross between a banana and a pineapple with some tropical fruit notes—and they grow wild, deep in the woods in Virginia! The cocktail wraps these tropical flavors around a rummy spirit base that's balanced with lime and then accented with Luxardo maraschino. For future mixing, a bar spoon of Luxardo is great way to add complexity and depth to fruity cocktails.

Yes, Mr. Washington

Shaken original

1½ OZ. LAIRD'S OLD APPLE BRANDY
1 OZ. CIDER REDUCTION (SEE APPENDIX)
1 TBSP. PUMPKIN BUTTER (SEE APPENDIX)
½ OZ. LEMON JUICE
½ OZ. EGG WHITE

Dry shake, then shake with ice. Double strain into a chilled cocktail coupe. Garnish with grated nutmeg.

This cocktail is a riff on our classic sour recipe (see the Whiskey Sour and the Clover Club). In this particular instance, we use an egg white not only for lightness and mouth feel, but also to solve a problem: we need to emulsify our pumpkin butter. If you remember from chapter 2, egg whites are the solution for a cocktail that settles, coagulates, or otherwise separates. The cider reduction and pumpkin butter work in tandem to adequately sweeten the drink.

2 oz. rum (spirit)	→	1½ oz. apple brandy (spirit)
½ oz. simple syrup (sweet)	→	1 oz. cider reduction 1 tbsp. pumpkin butter (sweet)
½ oz. lime juice (sour)	→	½ oz. lemon juice (sour)
		½ oz. egg white (length, mouth feel, emulsification)

TASTING NOTES: This cocktail tastes like the first sip of fall: apple brandy, sweetened with cider and spiced pumpkin, balanced with lemon, and lightened and emulsified with egg white. When the heat breaks in early October here in the mountains of Virginia, this is what you want to be drinking.

Unwed Sailor

Shaken original

1¾ OZ. MAKER'S MARK BOURBON
1 OZ. PECAN ORGEAT (SEE APPENDIX)
¾ OZ. PEDRO XIMÉNEZ SHERRY
½ OZ. LEMON JUICE
¼ OZ. ST. ELIZABETH ALLSPICE DRAM
2 GRAPEFRUIT QUARTER-WHEELS

Muddle grapefruit in shaker. Shake and double strain into a chilled cocktail coupe. Garnish with a grapefruit twist.

This is a mash-up of two classic cocktails, the Lion's Tail and the Ancient Mariner. In the former, bourbon is paired with citrus and allspice, and in the latter, dark rum is paired with allspice and grapefruit. I really wanted a darkly flavored, nutty bourbon cocktail with bright notes of grapefruit and spice for our winter drink list, and came to the above recipe. The pecan orgeat (an orgeat is a nut syrup) has just under half the sweetness of simple syrup, hence the full ounce. Similarly sherry is there for just a hint of sweetness, but also length.

Tasting notes: This is a winter-spiced cocktail where bourbon is complemented by the nuttiness in the pecan orgeat and sherry, balanced with lemon, and brightened with grapefruit, with just a hint of spice and bitter coming from the allspice dram. Pedro Ximénez (a style of rich, nutty sherry) is great for length and an extra hint of sweetness when you're looking to add depth to a cocktail, especially cocktails that feature aged distillates.

2 oz. rum (spirit)	→	1¾ oz. bourbon (spirit)
½ oz. simple syrup (sweet)	→	1 oz. pecan orgeat (sweet) ¾ oz. Pedro Ximénez sherry (sweet, length)
½ oz. lime juice (sour)	→	½ oz. lemon juice (sour)
		¼ oz. allspice dram (sweet, bitter, complexity) Grapefruit (complexity)

Hombre Concombre

Shaken original

1 OZ. DON JULIO BLANCO TEQUILA
1 OZ. DOLIN BLANC VERMOUTH
¾ OZ. PINEAPPLE CORDIAL (SEE APPENDIX)
½ OZ. LIME JUICE
1-INCH PIECE OF ENGLISH CUCUMBER

Muddle cucumber in shaker. Shake and double strain into a chilled cocktail coupe. Garnish with a cucumber slice.

I love Don Julio Blanco. I think that it and other rich blanco tequilas taste like roasted pineapple, melon, and cucumber, and consequently, they pair well with, ahem, pineapple, melon, and cucumber. I used Dolin Blanc (a rich white vermouth with vanilla notes that pairs nicely with berries and melons) in place of part of the spirit portion of this cocktail because I really wanted it to be just a tad lower in alcohol to let the subtle pineapple and cucumber flavors play throughout the drink. Notice that we have both pineapple cordial (a sweet component) and Dolin Blanc (length, sweet, and bitter) in the drink. Dolin does add sweetness, but it balances that with bitterness, keeping the drink from being too sweet with both sour (lime) and bitter (vermouth) present.

Tasting notes: This tastes like the cocktail essence of a rich blanco tequila: pineapple and cucumber supported by a distillate that echoes these same flavors, balanced with lime, lengthened and slightly bittered with a rich white vermouth. My wife hates tequila and loves this cocktail.

2 oz. rum (spirit)	→	1 oz. tequila (spirit)
½ oz. simple syrup (sweet)	→	¾ oz. pineapple cordial (sweet) 1 oz. Dolin Blanc (length, sweet, bitter, complexity)
½ oz. lime juice (sour)	→	½ oz. lime juice (sour)
		Cucumber (complexity)

Rose Hill Ruby

Shaken original

1¼ OZ. VITAE PLATINUM RUM
1 OZ. HIDALGO MANZANILLA PASTRANA SHERRY
¾ OZ. RHUBARB SYRUP (SEE APPENDIX)
½ OZ. GUAVA CORDIAL (SEE APPENDIX)
½ OZ. LIME JUICE
1 GRAPEFRUIT QUARTER-WHEEL

Shake and double strain into a chilled cocktail coupe. Garnish with a lime wheel.

IF YOU RECALL from chapter 1, it makes the most sense to think about distillates not in terms of what they're made from but rather how much of the flavor of the original ferment shows up in the final distillate. This rum distinctly tastes like the molasses it's made from, and stands in contrast to lighter Bacardi-style rums. This rum has serious flavor. As such, a short shot of it goes a long way. Here we've riffed on a Daiquiri with a little length coming from a tart manzanilla sherry, and our sweet component is rhubarb syrup paired with guava cordial. And on a technical note, one of my favorite tricks for getting a hint of citrus in a shaken cocktail is throwing a wedge or wheel in the shaker.

TASTING NOTES: To me, rhubarb in an interesting crossover fruit-veggie. It's celery-like, with tart apple and tannins on the palate. It's been historically paired with fruit to bring out its fruitier side, and I like to pair it with watermelon, strawberry, and . . . guava! Guava screams tropical fruit, so making a rum cocktail is where I ended up when riffing on these flavors. The short shot of Vitae creates a flavorful spirit backbone, the tart sherry accents the apple flavors in the rhubarb, and the guava and lime round out and balance the drink. And finally, the hint of grapefruit adds another layer of depth to the chord on the palate.

2 oz. rum (spirit)	→	1¼ oz. rum (spirit)
½ oz. simple syrup (sweet)	→	¾ oz. rhubarb syrup ½ oz. guava cordial (sweet)
½ oz. lime juice (sour)	→	½ oz. lime juice (sour)
		1 oz. manzanilla sherry (length, complexity) Grapefruit (complexity)

12 Monkeys

Shaken original

1½ OZ. STRANGE MONKEY GIN
1½ OZ. WATERMELON JUICE
¾ OZ. STRAWBERRY CORDIAL (SEE APPENDIX)
½ OZ. LIME JUICE
¼ OZ. CAMPARI

Shake and double strain into a chilled cocktail coupe. Garnish with a watermelon spear.

IN CHAPTER 2, we talked about using lengtheners to add flavor and dilute the booziness of concentrated cocktails. Here we have a gin Daiquiri riff with strawberry cordial for our sweet component, Campari for complexity and a hint of bitter, and watermelon for length and flavor.

2 oz. rum (spirit)	→	1½ oz. gin (spirit)
½ oz. simple syrup (sweet)	→	¾ oz. strawberry cordial (sweet)
½ oz. lime juice (sour)	→	½ oz. lime juice (sour)
		1½ oz. watermelon juice (length, complexity) ¼ oz. Campari (bitter, complexity)

TASTING NOTES: This is a perfect July cocktail: ripe watermelon lengthening a lightly floral gin Daiquiri flavored with strawberries. If you remember from the recipe for the Carpetbagger, picking a ¼ oz. of the right bittersweet cordial can complement and elevate fruit and herb flavors in shaken cocktails, and here we have a scant ¼ oz. of Campari smartly paired with watermelon and strawberry. The lime balances our booze and sugar, and the hint of bitterness coming from Campari is the last note on the palate, whetting your taste buds for another sip of summer in a glass.

Basil Leaf

Shaken original

1¾ OZ. STOLICHNAYA VODKA
1¾ OZ. CANTALOUPE JUICE
½ OZ. SIMPLE SYRUP
½ OZ. LIME JUICE
¼ OZ. CONTRATTO BIANCO VERMOUTH
5 BASIL LEAVES

Shake and double strain into a chilled cocktail coupe. Garnish with a basil leaf.

In chapter 1, we talked about how neutral spirits are a good fit for delicate flavors that are easily overwhelmed. In midsummer melons are perfectly ripe, fragrant, and delicious, and I wanted to try to capture those delicate flavors in a glass. Here I'm riffing on a vodka Daiquiri, lengthened with cantaloupe and accented with white vermouth and basil.

2 oz. rum (spirit)	→	1¾ oz. vodka (spirit)
½ oz. simple syrup (sweet)	→	½ oz. simple syrup (sweet)
½ oz. lime juice (sour)	→	½ oz. lime juice (sour)
		1¾ oz. cantaloupe juice (length, complexity) ¼ oz. Contratto Bianco (bitter, complexity) Basil (complexity)

Tasting notes: This cocktail tastes like sucking up a ripe piece of fresh melon. Vodka gives us an alcohol backbone without overwhelming the melon flavors, lime balances the sugar, and fresh basil and white vermouth add notes in the middle and finish of the cocktail, respectively. Contratto Bianco is perfect for adding a delicate white-raisin bitter finish that makes you go back for another sip.

Meyer LeMon

Shaken original

1¾ OZ. TANQUERAY RANGPUR GIN
1 OZ. MEYER LEMON CORDIAL (SEE APPENDIX)
1 TSP. MEYER LEMON CONFIT (SEE APPENDIX)
½ OZ. DOLIN BLANC VERMOUTH
½ OZ. EGG WHITE
¼ OZ. PASSION FRUIT CORDIAL (SEE APPENDIX)

Dry shake, then shake with ice. Double strain into a chilled cocktail coupe. Garnish with a bitters swirl.

MEYER LEMONS ARE PRETTY COOL. They have the same acidic profile as regular lemons, but they also have some additional notes of mandarin and orange, especially in the oil in the peels. Here we have a Daiquiri riff with a citrusy gin as the spirit base, combined with a cordial that includes the sour and part of the sweet component in one ingredient, much like in the Gimlet. I added a fat teaspoon of Meyer lemon confit to reinforce that Meyer lemon flavor and to shore up our sweet component. Dolin Blanc is there for length and complexity, egg white keeps the drink emulsified and light on the palate, and a scant ¼ oz. of passion fruit cordial accents the orange and mandarin notes in the Meyer lemon. This is one of the more technical cocktails presented in this book, but I'm hoping that you've learned enough by now to realize this cocktail is just a fancy Daiquiri riff with egg white, lengtheners, and flavor accents.

2 oz. rum (spirit)	→	1¾ oz. gin (spirit)
½ oz. simple syrup (sweet)	→	¼ oz. passion fruit cordial (sweet, complexity) 1 tsp. Meyer lemon confit (sweet)
½ oz. lime (sour)	→	1 oz. Meyer lemon cordial (sweet and sour)
		½ oz. Dolin Blanc (length, sweet, bitter, complexity) ½ oz. egg white (length, mouth feel)

TASTING NOTES: This cocktail tastes like the fortified essence of a Meyer lemon. Tanqueray Rangpur has bright citrus notes that pair seamlessly with the Meyer lemon cordial and confit. Dolin Blanc brings a soft, vanilla bittersweetness that keeps the drink lengthened and the sour component from being too aggressive. Egg white similarly softens the sour components, emulsifies the confit, and lightens the mouth feel.

Kentucky Alexander

Shaken original using fat/savory

2 OZ. MAKER'S MARK BOURBON
2 TBSP. SALTED RUM CARAMEL (SEE APPENDIX)
1½ OZ. HEAVY CREAM
½ OZ. EGG WHITE

Dry shake, then shake with ice. Double strain into a chilled cocktail coupe. Garnish with black sea salt.

As we mentioned briefly in chapter 1, a savory/fatty ingredient can be used in place of sour/bitter to balance our two other requisite cocktail components, spirit and sweet. Here we use a rich salted rum caramel and cream in place of a sour/bitter ingredient to foil our booze and sugar. It's a minimally reworked Whiskey Sour, with the caramel and cream taking the place of the lemon juice.

2 oz. bourbon (spirit)	→	2 oz. bourbon (spirit)
¾ oz. simple syrup (sweet)	→	2 tbsp. salted rum caramel (sweet, fatty/savory)
¾ oz. lemon (sour)	→	1½ oz. heavy cream (fatty/savory)
½ oz. egg white (length, mouthfeel)	→	½ oz. egg white (length, mouthfeel)

TASTING NOTES: This cocktail reminds me of the rare holiday bourbon balls of my youth: a hint of caramel corn alcohol warmth, enveloped in a casing of rich caramel cream, with just a hint of salt. This drink attests to the efficacy of fat and salt in standing up to and complementing booze and sugar.

Prohibition, the Death of Technique, and the Idiot-Proof Cocktail: The Highball

When Prohibition hit in 1920, many of the skilled bartenders of America didn't choose different occupations in the U.S.; they left the country. A grand and tragic amount of industry and professional know-how was lost. When Prohibition was repealed in 1933, the Thomasian professionalism of guest experience, technical proficiency, and encyclopedic knowledge of recipes was replaced by something else: the bottom line. Legitimate American businesses had missed out on the profits from selling booze for over a decade, and they needed to move some units with unskilled laborers. Enter the highball.

The highball is the natural capitalist response to the labor intensiveness of the "cock-tail," simply a built cocktail with two ingredients that can be made quickly so as to serve more people—and move more units! Examples include the rum and Coke, gin and tonic, vodka-cranberry, and so on and so forth. Their construction is so simple that a teetotaling Pentecostal kid like me could make them, and the minimal effort and knowledge they require makes them the common currency of mixed drinks in most contemporary, nonfancy cocktail bars. These drinks *do follow the same theoretical rules as cocktails* (they need our three components, spirit-sweet-sour/bitter), and they can be delicious when made with quality ingredients. The basic structure for a highball is just one part spirit plus two to three parts mixer, combined in a highball glass with ice. Essentially it's the most stripped-down possible variation on our shaken archetype, the Daiquiri, though as I mentioned highballs are typically built in the glass rather than shaken.

2 oz. rum (spirit)	→	2 oz. spirit (spirit)
½ oz. simple syrup (sweet)	→	4-6 oz. mixer (sweet, sour, length)
½ oz. lime juice (sour)	→	

The mixers for most highballs contain significant quantities of sugar as well as acidity (and sometimes bitterness; e.g., tonic water), so they function as both the sweet *and* the sour/bitter components in the cocktail. Highballs are *not* technically demanding—which is great when you're faced with a bartender as ignorant as I was when I started mixing years ago! And despite having cultivated a taste for fancy things, I certainly don't hate on a Bourbon 'n' Ginger from time to time.

4

MAKING YOUR OWN SIGNATURE COCKTAILS

In the previous three chapters, we laid a theoretical framework for approaching cocktails, we discussed our requisite components in detail, we introduced tools and the core technical knowledge for correctly preparing cocktails, and we related a whole cadre of classic and original cocktails to shaken and stirred archetypes. Where do we go from here? Well, young bartender, it's time for you to leave the nest, spread your wings, and start riffing on cocktails on your own.

What? You feel overwhelmed? You shouldn't! Remember our plan of attack: pick a successful scaffold, classify your ingredients, substitute like ingredient for like ingredient to be certain all of our requisite categories—spirit, sweet, sour/bitter—are represented, and put your own finishing touches on your creation. The tables that follow start with a successful scaffold and then list many of the methods we've used in this book to manipulate a classic recipe into a new creation. Use them to create your own signature cocktails!

Choose Your Own Adventure: Stirred Cocktail

Pick a Cocktail Scaffold	Classify Your Ingredients	Sub in a Spirit (or Spirits) for Rye	Sub in bitter and sweet ingredients for Vermouth
Manhattan	Rye (spirit) Vermouth (sweet, bitter) Cocktail bitters (bitter, complexity)	**VODKA** **GIN** London dry Old Tom Plymouth American/other **RUM** Rum Rhum agricole Cachaça **WHISK(E)Y** Bourbon Scotch **MEZCAL** Mezcal Tequila **FRUIT DISTILLATES** Grape brandy Apple brandy Grappa Pisco	**A&F WINES** Carpano Antica Punt e Mes Contratto Rosso Cocchi Torino Contratto Bianco Dolin Blanc Dolin Dry Byrrh Cocchi Americano Cappelletti Lillet Blanc Elisir Novasalus **BITTERSWEET CORDIALS** Fernet Branca Branca Menta Campari Absinthe Maraschino Yellow Chartreuse Green Chartreuse Amaro Nonino Zucca Allspice dram Root Bénédictine Cynar

ADDITIONAL COMPLEXITY VIA COCKTAIL BITTERS?	TOO BITTER? BALANCE WITH SWEET	EXECUTE TECHNIQUE
Angostura Angostura orange Peychaud's Bob's Abbott's Bob's peppermint Micah's lavender Micah's spiced orange Micah's cherry sassafras	**SYRUP** Simple syrup Honey syrup Cider reduction Birch syrup **LIQUEURS AND CORDIALS** Cointreau Dry curaçao	Build in mixing glass or tin Add ice Stir for thirty seconds Single strain into chilled cocktail glass Add additional complexity with a garnish

Choose Your Own Adventure: Shaken Cocktail			
Pick a cocktail scaffold	**Classify your ingredients**	**Sub in a spirit (or spirits) for rum**	**Sub in one or more sweet ingredients for simple syrup**
Daiquiri	Rum (spirit) Simple syrup (sweet) Lime (sour)	**VODKA** **GIN** London dry Old Tom Plymouth American/ other **RUM** Rum Rhum agricole Cachaça **WHISK(E)Y** Bourbon Rye Scotch **MEZCAL** Mezcal Tequila **FRUIT DISTILLATES** Grape brandy Apple brandy Grappa Pisco **LIQUEURS/CORDIALS** Cointreau Dry curaçao	**FLAVORED SYRUPS** Birch syrup Cider reduction Rhubarb syrup Honey syrup Orgeat Orange confit Meyer lemon confit Pumpkin butter Oleo saccharum **MACERATED FRUIT CORDIALS** Macerated peaches Pineapple cordial Strawberry cordial Paw paw cordial Cranberry cordial Guava cordial Passion fruit cordial Raspberry cordial

Sub in one or more sour ingredients for lime	Add additional complexity?		Execute technique
Lemon Lime	**ACCENT WITH BITTERSWEET CORDIALS** *(bitter, sweet)* Fernet Branca Amaro Nonino Branca Menta Zucca Campari Allspice dram Absinthe Root Maraschino Bénédictine Yellow Chartreuse Cynar Green Chartreuse **ACCENT WITH A&F WINES** *(bitter, sweet)* Carpano Antica Byrrh	**ACCENT WITH COCKTAIL BITTERS** *(bitter)* Angostura Angostura orange Peychaud's Bob's Abbott's Bob's peppermint Micah's lavender Micah's spiced orange Micah's cherry sassafras **LENGTHENERS** Fruit juice Fortified wines Soda	Build in mixing glass/tin Dry shake (if needed) Add ice Shake for twelve seconds Double strain into chilled cocktail glass
SWEET AND SOUR INGREDIENTS Lime cordial Meyer lemon cordial	Punt e Mes Cocchi Americano Contratto Rosso Cappelletti Cocchi Torino Lillet Blanc Elisir Novasalus Contratto Bianco Dolin Blanc Dolin Dry	Wine Tea Sparkling wine Egg white Beer **ADDITIONAL COMPLEXITY VIA** Muddled fruit Herbs Garnish Sprinkles!	

Appendix I

Bitters, Cordials & Other Preparations

Birch Syrup

2 POUNDS BLACK BIRCH STICKS, CUT INTO SMALL PIECES (LESS THAN 3 INCHES)
2 GALLONS COLD WATER
2 CUPS SUGAR
2 CUPS HONEY

Add birch sticks to water and steep overnight, or for at least 12 hours. Cold-steeped tea should be fragrant, smelling of wintergreen and tobacco. Heat sticks and water and bring to a boil. Boil for 15 minutes, then strain out birch sticks and discard them. Reduce birch-infused tea to a final volume of around 1 quart. This will take at least 1 hour. Strain tea through a coffee filter and then add sugar, stirring until dissolved. Add honey and stir to incorporate. Once sugar and honey are dissolved, refrigerate syrup. Should keep for 1 month or more.

BASIC BITTERS RECIPE

1 TSP. OR MORE BITTERING AGENT (CINCHONA, WORMWOOD, GENTIAN, ETC.)
PRIMARY FLAVORING AGENT
COMPLEMENTARY FLAVORING AGENTS
1½ CUP HIGH-PROOF, NEUTRAL SPIRIT (EVERCLEAR, SMIRNOFF 100, OR OTHERS)
SYRUP TO TASTE

Combine bittering and flavoring agents in a clean Mason jar and add spirit. Infuse for 10 days. After 10 days, separate solids from infused spirit, setting the spirit aside. Place solids in a saucepan and add just enough water to cover. Bring mixture to a boil, then remove from heat and allow to cool. Pour cooled mixture into a second Mason jar and infuse for another 10 days. After 10 days, strain solids and combine infused water with infused spirit. Strain mixture through a coffee filter, and then sweeten to taste.

After straining the infusion the first time, I taste it to make sure that my main flavoring agent is the top note on the palate. If not, I shore up the main flavor by adding another measure of the primary flavoring agent to the infused spirit after straining the solids from it. I do that with all three recipes below.

MICAH'S CHERRY SASSAFRAS BITTERS

2 cups frozen sweet cherries	Primary flavoring agent
1-inch piece of vanilla bean	Secondary flavoring agents
1 cinnamon stick	
1 tbsp. juniper berries	
1 tbsp. whole mace blades	
Peels from 1 orange	
2 star anise pods	
1 tsp. cloves	
½ tsp. wild cherry bark	Bittering agents
⅛ tsp. ground cinchona	
2 tsp. sassafras root	
1½ cups Smirnoff 100	High-proof, neutral spirit
2 tbsp. 2:1 demerara syrup	Syrup to taste

MICAH'S LAVENDER BITTERS

1 cup fresh lavender flowers (dried flowers also work in a pinch)	Primary flavoring agent
Peels from 3 lemons	Secondary flavoring agents
Peels from 1 orange	
2 tbsp. whole cardamom	
2 sprigs fresh hyssop	
1 tsp. pink peppercorns	
1 tsp. juniper	
1 star anise pod	
¾ tsp. whole gentian	Bittering agents
¼ tsp. licorice root	
½ tsp. calamus	
1½ cups Smirnoff 100	High-proof, neutral spirit
3 tbsp. 2:1 simple syrup	Syrup to taste

MICAH'S ORANGE SPICE BITTERS

Peels from 7 oranges	Primary flavoring agent
6 cloves	Secondary flavoring agents
1 tbsp. cardamom	
½ tsp. juniper	
1 star anise pod	
1 cinnamon stick	
2 fresh bay leaves	
½ tsp. Indian sarsaparilla	Bittering agents
¼ tsp. gentian	
½ tsp. calamus	
2 cup Smirnoff 100	High-proof, neutral spirit
3 tbsp. 1:1 demerara syrup	Syrup to taste

Campari Sprinkles

2 CUPS CAMPARI
1 TSP. CORNSTARCH
2 TBSP. SUGAR

Combine Campari, cornstarch, and sugar in a saucepan. Bring to a boil, stirring until sugar and cornstarch dissolve. Remove from heat. Pour mixture onto a lined baking sheet (a silicon baking liner works best). Preheat oven to 200° F and cook for 2 hours, or until Campari mixture starts to bubble and dehydrate. Allow to cool and then crumble into sprinkles. Store in a dry, cool place.

Cider Reduction

6 CUPS APPLE CIDER
1 CINNAMON STICK
1 CLOVE
½ CUP BROWN SUGAR

Bring cider and spices to a boil until reduced to 2 cups. Strain out spices and add brown sugar, stirring to dissolve. Allow syrup to cool before using. Because this syrup is heavily cooked, it can be frozen without significant loss of flavor. Refrigerate the portion you opt not to freeze. Should keep for 1 month or more.

Cranberry Cordial

12 OZ. FRESH CRANBERRIES
3½ CUPS WATER
2¾ CUPS SUGAR
½ TSP. CITRIC ACID
4 CLOVES
1 CINNAMON STICK
1-INCH PIECE OF VANILLA BEAN
4 CARDAMOM PODS
PEELS FROM 2 ORANGES
¼ CUP BRANDY

Combine all ingredients except orange peels and brandy and bring to a boil. Reduce heat and simmer for 15 minutes, until cranberries are soft. Remove from heat, add orange peels, and steep for 15 minutes. Remove cinnamon stick and orange peels and coarsely blend syrup with an immersion blender. Strain hot syrup through a strainer lined with a dish towel. Allow syrup to cool and then add brandy. Overcooking syrup will result in a jelly-like cordial. Keep refrigerated. Should keep for 2 months or more.

Guava Cordial

1 KG. (2.2 LB.) GUAVA PURÉE
2 CUPS SUGAR
1 CUP DRY, UNOAKED WHITE WINE

Blend purée with sugar and wine until sugar dissolves and cordial has a uniform texture. Keep refrigerated. Should keep for 1 month or more.

Habanero Tincture

8 HABANERO PEPPERS, THINLY SLICED
1 CUP VODKA

Combine vodka and habaneros in a Mason jar and infuse for 7 days. Strain out peppers and run tincture through a coffee filter. Store in a clean jar or bottle at room temperature. Will last for 1 year or more.

Lime Cordial

12 LIMES
1 CUP SUGAR
1 CUP WATER
1 TSP. CITRIC ACID
¼ TSP. TARTARIC ACID

Zest limes. Cut zested limes in half and juice using an enamel or motorized citrus reamer. Reserve juice; should yield close to 2 cups. Combine sugar and acids with water and bring to a boil. Remove from heat and steep lime zest in hot syrup for 15 minutes. Strain zest from syrup and allow syrup to cool. Add cooled syrup to lime juice. Keep refrigerated. With the additional sugar and acidity, the cordial will stay freshly limey for 7–10 days.

Macerated Peaches

4 CUPS PEACHES, PITTED AND CUT INTO QUARTERS
1½ CUPS SUGAR

Place peaches in a container and sprinkle with sugar, stirring to coat evenly. Cover and leave for at least 1 hour. Most of the sugar should dissolve. The peaches will lose much of their fragrance and flavor after 2 or 3 days. Refrigerate after macerating.

Meyer Lemon Confit

10 MEYER LEMONS
SUGAR
WATER

Rinse lemons thoroughly and peel, being careful to get as little pith as possible. (If you get a lot of pith, use a paring knife to carefully remove it.) In a saucepan, combine peels with enough ice-cold water to completely cover them. Bring to a boil, remove from heat, and strain peels from water. Repeat process a total of four times, using fresh cold water each time.

Cut peeled lemons in half and juice them with a citrus reamer. To calculate the amount of sugar needed, take the total volume of lemon juice and divide by 2. For example, if you have 1 cup of lemon juice, you'll need ½ cup of sugar. Combine juice and sugar with peels in a saucepan and stir to dissolve sugar. Bring mixture to a boil. Cook over medium heat for 45 minutes, until reduced by ½ to ⅓ of original volume.

Remove from heat and coarsely blend. Keep refrigerated. Should keep for 3 months or more.

Meyer Lemon Cordial

12 MEYER LEMONS
1 CUP SUGAR
1 CUP WATER
1 TSP. CITRIC ACID

Zest lemons. Cut zested lemons in half and juice using an enamel or motorized citrus reamer. Reserve juice; should yield close to 2 cups. Combine sugar and acid with water and bring to a boil. Remove from heat and steep lemon zest in hot syrup for 15 minutes. Strain zest from syrup and allow syrup to cool. Add cooled syrup to lemon juice. Keep refrigerated. With the additional sugar and acidity, the cordial will stay freshly lemony for 7–10 days.

Orange Confit

10 ORANGES
SUGAR
WATER

Rinse oranges thoroughly and peel, being careful to get as little pith as possible. (If you get a lot of pith, use a paring knife to carefully remove it.) In a saucepan, combine peels with enough ice-cold water to completely cover them. Bring to a boil, remove from heat, and strain peels from water. Repeat process a total of four times, using fresh cold water each time.

Cut peeled oranges in half and juice them with a citrus reamer. To calculate the amount of sugar needed, take the total volume of orange juice and divide by 3. For example, if you have 3 cups of orange juice, you'll need 1 cup of sugar. Combine juice and sugar with peels in a saucepan and stir to dissolve the sugar. Bring this mixture to a boil. Cook over medium heat for 45 minutes, until reduced by ½ to ⅓ of original volume.

Remove from heat and coarsely blend. Keep refrigerated. Should keep for 3 months or more.

Passion Fruit Cordial

1 KG. (2.2 LB.) PASSION FRUIT PURÉE
2 CUPS SUGAR
1 CUP DRY, UNOAKED WHITE WINE

Blend purée with sugar and wine until sugar dissolves and cordial has a uniform texture. Keep refrigerated. Should keep for 1 month or more.

Paw Paw Cordial

PAW PAWS
SUGAR
DRY, UNOAKED WHITE WINE

Peel paw paws with a paring knife. Scoop out flesh and seeds. Using a stock strainer and a wooden reamer, ream seeds and flesh to push flesh through strainer. Combine four parts seeded paw paw flesh with two parts sugar and one part wine, then blend until sugar is dissolved and cordial has a uniform texture. The essence of paw paws is fleeting; try to use the cordial in a day or two.

Pecan Orgeat

2½ CUPS WATER
1½ CUPS PECANS
½ CUP SUGAR
½ CUP BROWN SUGAR
¼ CUP AGED RUM

Toast pecans in a dry skillet until fragrant. Combine pecans with water in a Vitamix or blender and blend thoroughly. Allow pecan-water mixture to sit at room temperature for 6–12 hours, and then strain through a dinner napkin or cheesecloth. Take up the ends of the cloth and wring as much nut milk as possible out of nut solids. Should yield about 2 cups pecan milk. In a saucepan, add sugars and pecan milk and heat gently to dissolve sugars, being careful not to bring the mixture to a boil. Once sugar is dissolved, remove from heat, allow orgeat to cool, add rum, and refrigerate. The orgeat should keep for about 3 weeks in the refrigerator and will be just under half as sweet as simple syrup. Keep that in mind when substituting orgeat for other sweet components.

Pineapple Cordial

1 LARGE PINEAPPLE, PEELED AND CHOPPED, APPROXIMATELY 4 CUPS
2 CUPS SUGAR
1 CUP DRY, UNOAKED WHITE WINE

Place pineapple in a container and sprinkle with sugar, stirring to coat evenly. Cover and let sit for at least an hour, or until much of the sugar is dissolved into a rich syrup. Add wine and stir to help dissolve remaining sugar. Using an immersion blender, coarsely blend the macerated pineapple-wine mixture. Strain through a chinois. Keep refrigerated. Should keep for 1 month or more.

Pumpkin Butter

4 SUGAR PUMPKINS
¾ CUP DR PEPPER
¾ CUP BROWN SUGAR
1 CUP SUGAR
1½ TSP. CINNAMON
½ TSP. NUTMEG
¼ TSP. CLOVES
¼ TSP. ALLSPICE

Cut tops off pumpkins and cut pumpkins in half. Remove seeds. Roast pumpkins face down on a sheet pan at 350° F for about 1 hour, or until the flesh can be easily scraped away from the shell. Allow pumpkins to cool, and then scrape out the flesh.

Use a microplane to grate the nutmeg. Grind allspice, cloves, and cinnamon in a spice grinder, and add spices, sugar, and Dr Pepper to pumpkin flesh. In a large pot or Dutch oven, cook this mixture for roughly 1 hour over medium heat, stirring frequently, and season with additional sugar and spice to taste. Purée the pumpkin mixture in batches in a Vitamix or blender until smooth.

This recipe yields all the pumpkin butter I need for the fall (about 4 quarts or more), so scale it down to your needs. Should keep 1 month refrigerated; any extra can be frozen.

Raspberry Cordial

2 CUPS FRESH RASPBERRIES
1 CUP SUGAR
½ CUP DRY, UNOAKED WHITE WINE OR ROSÉ WINE

Stir sugar into berries and let macerate for at least 1 hour. Add wine and stir to dissolve remaining sugar. Strain through a chinois. Keep refrigerated. Should keep for 1 month or more.

Rhubarb Syrup

1 LB. RHUBARB, APPROXIMATELY 4 CUPS CHOPPED
2 CUPS SUGAR
2 CUPS WATER
½ TSP. CITRIC ACID
¼ TSP. MALIC ACID
PEELS OF 2 GRAPEFRUITS
¼ CUP VODKA

Trim any leaves off rhubarb and chop stalks coarsely. Combine stalks, sugar, acids, and water in a saucepan. Bring to a boil, then simmer for 20 minutes. Remove from heat and steep grapefruit peels in hot syrup for 15 minutes. Strain solids and peels from syrup using a chinois. Allow syrup to cool, then add vodka. Keep refrigerated. Should keep for up to 3 weeks.

Salted Rum Caramel

2 CUPS SUGAR
2 CUPS CREAM
1 CUP WATER
½ TSP. SALT
¼ CUP DARK RUM

Combine sugar and salt in a saucepan with water and bring to a boil. Continue boiling until syrup takes on a copper-penny color as sugar caramelizes, then remove from heat. Slowly add cream, keeping in mind that it will initially boil vigorously. Allow caramel to cool for a few minutes, then add rum. Keep refrigerated. Should last 1 month or more.

Strawberry Cordial

1 KG. (2.2 LB.) STRAWBERRY PURÉE
2 CUPS SUGAR
1 CUP DRY, UNOAKED WHITE WINE OR ROSÉ WINE

Blend purée with sugar and wine until sugar dissolves and cordial has a uniform texture. Keep refrigerated. Should keep for 1 month or more.

Appendix 2

Commonly Used Terms behind the Bar

Bar spoon: The amount of liquid that can fit in a bar spoon, about ⅛ oz. or 4 ml.

Bus: To clean a table or seat thoroughly to prepare for the arrival of the next guest.

Dash: Approximately ¹⁄₃₆ oz. or .8 ml.

Dead: Indicates that something is no longer needed and can be put back in its place; e.g., "Is this Carpano on your station dead?"

Double: Twice the volume of a single shot.

Drop: Approximately .05 ml.; about 16 drops equals 1 dash.

Dry: Asking for a dry Martini used to mean that you wanted a hefty pour of vermouth—originally two parts gin to one part vermouth. Over the years, the sense of the term *dry* has become inverted to mean that a patron would like *less* vermouth than in a standard Martini—so much so that asking for an extra dry Martini means that the bartender will generally avoid adding any at all. I have had cocktail nerds ask me for a dry Martini in the original sense recently, and I have a sneaking suspicion that the phrase will come full circle in the years to come.

Eighty-six: This number indicates that an item, practice, or person is no longer available; e.g. "Eighty-six Maker's Mark sub Elijah Craig for Old Fashioneds tonight."

Fat: Just above the specified quantity; e.g., a fat ¼ oz. is just more than ¼ oz., but less than ½ oz.

Fifth: A 750 ml. bottle, approximately one-fifth of a gallon. Fifths are the most common bottle size behind most bars.

HANDLE: A 1,750 ml. or approximately half-gallon bottle of liquor; so called because they often have handles.

HOLD: Omit; e.g., "I'll have a shot of Don Julio Blanco, hold the fruit."

IN THE WEEDS: When the amount of work coming into a work station exceeds the maximum output of the station and overwhelms the worker. For example, if I can make three cocktails per minute, and I get five orders for three drinks apiece in a single minute, I'll be in the weeds for a good five minutes or more. Being in the weeds is a source of great anxiety for folks in the biz, and a steady source of restaurant anxiety dreams.

JIGGER: Refers to a measuring cup or a measured shot of spirit.

NEAT: A spirit served right out of the bottle into a glass—usually a tumbler or rocks glass—with no ice.

ON THE FLY: Indicates that something is needed as soon as possible; e.g., "I need a Manhattan on the fly" or "I need you to bus seat 16 on the fly."

PERFECT: Describes a cocktail in which the vermouth portion is split evenly between sweet and dry; e.g., a perfect Manhattan is made with 2 oz. rye, ½ oz. sweet vermouth, ½ oz. dry vermouth, and a dash of bitters. "Perfect" drinks are frequently served with a lemon twist.

PHONE CHARGER: Something you should never ask your bartender for.

RESTAURANT ANXIETY DREAMS: A dream in which a series of worst-case in-the-weeds scenarios overlap; e.g., a hundred people walk in at the same time and you're the only bartender, and you realize you don't have any glassware and can't find anything. I've only recently stopped getting these.

ROCKS: Ice cubes.

SERVICE: Refers to the hours in which dinner and drinks are served; e.g., "We were in the weeds for the entire service tonight."

SHOT: The amount of spirit that would go into a cocktail, around 1½ to 2 oz., usually served neat; e.g., "I'll have a Budweiser and shot of Buffalo Trace."

SINGLE: A single shot of spirit, usually between 1½ to 2 oz.

STRAIGHT UP: Lots of folks use *straight up* (or just *up*) incorrectly. That is, they use *straight up* when the really mean *neat;* they want a shot of spirit straight out of a bottle. Others use *straight up* and *up* correctly to indicate that they want a stirred cocktail served in a Martini glass or stemmed coupe as opposed to in a tumbler. I interpret both *straight up* and *up* to mean that a patron would like a stirred cocktail served "up" in a cocktail coupe.

TALL: Indicates that a patron would like a highball cocktail in a larger or "tall" glass; e.g., a patron may ask for a "single-tall rum and Coke," indicating they would like a single shot in a larger glass with more Coke. On the other hand, a patron who asks for "a tall rum and Coke" is secretly hoping that you'll serve them a double shot and charge them for a single shot. I always disambiguate this by asking, "Would you like a single- or a double-tall?"

WET: The opposite of *dry* in reference to a Martini; i.e., a request for a wet Martini indicates that the patron would like more dry vermouth than in the standard drink. Again, as the classic dry Martini reclaims its semantic domain, we'll hear this word used less and less. In the meantime, use *wet* to request a classic 2:1 Martini.

WET ICE: The ice that was used to make a cocktail. Sometimes a patron will ask to have that ice served with the cocktail on the side; e.g., "I'll have a Beefeater Martini up with olives, wet ice on the side, please."

Notes

2. *Mr. Boston's bar book:* The *Mr. Boston Official Bartender's Guide,* a popular reference for home and professional bartenders since the 1930s.

7. *Research suggests lab animals avoid alcohol:* Adam Rogers, *Proof: The Science of Booze* (New York: Houghton Mifflin Harcourt, 2014), 147–49.

8. *History of Punch:* David Wondrich, *Punch: The Delights (and Dangers) of the Flowing Bowl* (New York: Penguin, 2010), 22, 27, 26, 51.

9. *Tea and citrus were luxury items:* Sarah Meacham, *Every Home a Distillery* (Baltimore: Johns Hopkins University Press, 2009), 7.

10. *Drunkenness and hangovers were a daily problem:* David Wondrich, *Imbibe! From Absinthe Cocktail to Whiskey Smash, a Salute in Stories and Drinks to "Professor" Jerry Thomas, Pioneer of the American Bar* (New York: Penguin, 2007), 149–51.

10. *Bitters added to treat hangovers:* Brad Parsons, *Bitters: A Spirited History of a Classic Cure-All* (Berkeley: Ten Speed Press, 2011), 9.

10. *First use of "cock-tail" in print:* Ibid., 8.

10. *Hot pokers and the modern palate:* Dave Arnold, *Liquid Intelligence: The Art and Science of the Perfect Cocktail* (New York: Norton), 177–79.

10. *Frederic Tudor's ice business:* Gavin Weightman, *The Frozen Water Trade: A True Story* (New York: Hyperion, 2007), 2.

10. *Effects of the ice trade on drinking culture:* Wondrich, *Imbibe!,* 40.

12. *Mixologists usher in golden age of cocktails:* Ibid., 40–49.

16. *Proof:* Proof as listed on a bottle nowadays is simply the ABV times two; e.g., a whiskey that is 40 percent ABV is 80 proof.

Proof, incidentally, was a term used by British sailors who sought to verify the strength of their daily ration of rum by adding gunpowder to it and then "proving" it, or putting a lit match to it. If the rum caught fire, it was of sufficient "proof." See Rogers, *Proof*, 92.

16. In these pages, spirits are defined in accordance with the United States Alcohol and Tobacco Tax and Trade Bureau's *Beverage Alcohol Manual*, chapter 4.

18. *Derivation of gin:* Lesley Jacobs Solomonson, *Gin: A Global History* (London: Reaktion Books, 2012), 23.

19. *Old Tom gin:* Wondrich, *Imbibe!*, 58–59.

22. *The tiki cocktail movement:* Jeff Berry, *Beach Bum Berry's Potions of the Carribean* (New York: Cocktail Kingdom, 2014), 158.

33. *Heat sensitivity of fruits and herbs:* Harold McGee, *On Food and Cooking: The Science and Lore of the Kitchen* (New York: Scribner, 2004), 397.

38. *Acidity of lime versus lemon juice:* Ibid., 376–77.

40. *Evolutionary history of bitterness:* Ibid., 258; Katherine Unger Baillie, "A Tale of Two Genes: Penn Team Elucidates Evolution of Bitter Taste Sensitivity," *Penn News,* 11 November 2013; Evan Lerner, "Penn Geneticists Help Show Bitter Taste Perception Is Not Just about Flavors," *Penn News*, 5 December 2011.

55. *The julep strainer gave way to the Hawthorne strainer:* Wondrich, *Imbibe!*, 44.

60. *The Fundamental Law of Chilled Drinks:* Arnold, *Liquid Intelligence,* 84.

62. *A thermodynamic peculiarity of alcohol-water solutions:* Ibid., 76–79, 97–98.

62. *Vacuum effect when shaking cocktails:* Ibid., 99.

65. *Introduction of stirring and the Blue Blazer cocktail:* Wondrich, *Imbibe!*, 147.

65. *Optimal temperature and dilution of a stirred cocktail:* Arnold, *Liquid Intelligence,* 105.

65. *Most chilling in first thirty seconds of stirring:* Dave Arnold, "Cocktail Science in General: Part 1 of 2," http://www.cooking issues.com/index.html%3Fp=4585.html.

68. *Ice crystals act as natural filter:* Arnold, *Liquid Intelligence,* 66–68.

70. *Thirty percent of a cocktail's volume from ice:* Ibid., 130–35.

70. *Improved Whiskey Cocktail:* An Old Fashioned variation adding maraschino and absinthe. For the other two drinks, see the recipes in chapter 3.

82. *Manhattans as early as the 1880s:* Wondrich, *Imbibe!,* 239.

94. *Rye replacing cognac in Sazerac:* Ibid., 201.

118. *Background on Cappelletti, Campari, and Aperol:* Haus Alpenz Wine and Spirits Portfolio, 2016 v. 1; Andrea Burgener, "Change in Beetle-Juice Recipe is Haunting the Purists," *Times* (South Africa), 5 December 2012, http://www.timeslive.co.za/opinion/columnists/2012/12/05/change-in-beetle-juice-recipe-is-haunting-the-purists.

123. *Carbonating a cocktail produces carbonic acid:* Nathan Myhrvold, *Modernist Cuisine: The Art and Science of Cooking,* vol. 2 (Bellevue, WA: Cooking Lab, 2011), 465.

170. *History of Prohibition:* See Ken Burns's excellent documentary on the era.

196. *Original meaning of dry Martini:* Wondrich, *Imbibe!,* 247.

Recommended Reading

Arnold, David. *Liquid Intelligence: The Art and Science of the Perfect Cocktail.* New York: Norton, 2014.

Baker, Charles H. *The Gentleman's Companion, or Around the World with Jigger, Beaker, and Flask.* New York: Derrydale Press, 1939.

Berry, Jeff. *Beachbum Berry's Potions of the Caribbean.* New York: Cocktail Kingdom, 2014.

Burns, Ken. *Prohibition.* Washington, D.C.: PBS, 2011. TV miniseries.

Craddock, Harry. *The Savoy Cocktail Book.* London: Pavilion Books, 2003.

Czarra, Fred. *Spices: A Global History.* London: Reaktion Books, 2009.

Kaplan, David, Nick Fauchald, and Alex Day. *Death & Co: Modern Classic Cocktails.* Berkeley: Ten Speed Press, 2010.

McGee, Harold. *On Food and Cooking: The Science and Lore of the Kitchen.* New York: Scribner, 2004.

Meacham, Sarah. *Every Home a Distillery.* Baltimore: Johns Hopkins University Press, 2009.

Morgenthaler, Jeffrey. *The Bar Book: Elements of Cocktail Technique.* San Francisco: Chronicle Books, 2014.

Myhrvold, Nathan. *Modernist Cuisine: The Art and Science of Cooking.* Bellevue, WA: Cooking Lab, 2011.

O'Neil, Darcy. *Fix the Pumps.* Ontario: self-published, 2010.

Page, Karen, and Andrew Dornenburg. *The Flavor Bible: The Essential Guide to Culinary Creativity, Based on the Wisdom of America's Most Imaginative Chefs.* New York: Little, Brown, 2008.

Parsons, Brad. *Bitters: A Spirited History of a Classic Cure-All.* Berkeley: Ten Speed Press, 2011.

Rogers, Adam. *Proof: The Science of Booze.* New York: Houghton Mifflin Harcourt, 2014.

Smiley, Ian. *Making Pure Corn Whiskey: A Professional Guide for Amateur and Micro-Distillers.* Canada: Amphora Society, 1999.

Solmonson, Lesley Jacobs. *Gin: A Global History.* London: Reaktion Books, 2012.

Stewart, Amy. *The Drunken Botanist.* New York City: Algonquin Books, 2013.

Thomas, Jerry. *A Bar-Tender's Guide: How to Mix Drinks.* New York: Dick & Fitzgerald, 1862.

Weightman, Gavin. *The Frozen Water Trade: A True Story.* New York: Hyperion, 2007.

Wondrich, David. *Imbibe! From Absinthe Cocktail to Whiskey Smash, a Salute in Stories and Drinks to "Professor" Jerry Thomas, Pioneer of the American Bar.* New York: Penguin, 2007.

———. *Punch: The Delights (and Dangers) of the Flowing Bowl.* New York: Penguin, 2010.

Index

absinthe, 70–71
ABV (alcohol by volume), 16
Airmail, 139
amaros, 49
Ancient Mariner, 156
aperitifs, 49
apple brandies, 30
apple brandy cocktails
    Corpse Reviver No. 1, 86–87
    Widow's Kiss, 90–91
    Yes, Mr. Washington, 154–55
Arnold, Dave, 10, 59–60, 65
aromatized and fortified wines, 36, 41–45, 49

bar spoons, 54, 196
bartending
    common terms in, 196–98
    Mr. Potato Head approach to, 14–15, 56, 81
    Prohibition and, 170

Basil Leaf, 164–65
Bee's Knees, 126–27
Bijou, 98–99
birch syrup, 180
bitter, as flavor/cocktail component, 12–15, 39–49, 181–84
bittersweet cordial cocktails
    Bijou, 98–99
    Blackfriar Cocktail, 110–11
    Bonsoni, 100–101
    Carpetbagger, 150–51
    Clover Club, 77, 132–33
    Corpse Reviver No. 2, 70, 142–43
    Dead Rosetti, 106–7
    Greater Antilles, 120–21
    Improved Toronto, 108–9
    Lion's Tail, 128–29, 156
    Martinez, 92–93
    Mean Old Man, 114–15
    Montmartre, 112–13

bittersweet cordial cocktails (*continued*)
    Negroni, 96–97
    Nelson County Gentleman, 122–23
    Orange Artichoke, 104–5
    Paw Paw Daiquiri, 152–53
    Sazerac, 48, 70, 94–95
    Talking Serpent, 116–17
    12 Monkeys, 162–63
    Unwed Sailor, 156–57
    Vieux Carré, 88–89
    Widow's Kiss, 90–91
bittersweet cordials, 36, 40, 46–47, 49
Blackfriar Cocktail, 110–11
Blue Blazer, 65
Bonsoni, 100–101
Bourbon Peach Sour, 148–49
bourbon whiskey cocktails
    Bourbon Peach Sour, 148–49
    Dead Rosetti, 106–7
    Kentucky Alexander, 168–69
    Lion's Tail, 128–29, 156
    Old Fashioned, 48, 58, 102–3
    Orange Artichoke, 104–5
    Unwed Sailor, 156–57
    Whiskey Sour, 63, 77, 130–31
bourbon whiskies, 27–28
brandies, 30–31
brandy cocktails
    Corpse Reviver No. 1, 86–87
    French 75, 138–39
    Sazerac, 48, 70, 94–95
    Sidecar, 134–35
    Vieux Carré, 88–89
    Widow's Kiss, 90–91
    Yes, Mr. Washington, 154–55

Campari sprinkles, 132, 185
Carpetbagger, 150–51
champagne cocktails
    French 75, 138–39
champagne flutes, 58
cherry sassafras bitters, Micah's, 102, 182
chilling, 59–61
cider reduction, 185
citrus, 37–39, 72, 74
citrus peel syrups, macerated, 35

Clover Club, 77, 132–33
cocktail bitters, 47–49
cocktail coupes, 58
cocktails
    historical approaches to, 8–10
    necessary components of, 12–15, 175–79
    rules of thumb for balance in, 33, 38
    taste of, 15–16, 40–41
    techniques for, 59–77
    tools for, 53–58
"cock-tails," 9–10, 12
cocktail shakers, 53–54, 61
collins glasses, 58
cooked syrups, 33, 180, 185, 194
cordials, 35–36, 46–47, 49, 186–88, 190–92, 194–95
Corpse Reviver No. 1, 86–87
Corpse Reviver No. 2, 70, 142–43
coupes, cocktail, 58
cranberry cordial, 186

Daiquiri, 13, 124–25

Dead Rosetti, 106–7
digestifs/digestives, 49
dilution, 59–61
dry shaking, 63–64

egg whites, 63–64, 77, 131

fat, as flavor/cocktail component, 13, 168–69
flavored syrups, 33–35, 180, 185, 194
flutes, champagne, 58
fortified wines, 36, 41–45, 49
French 75, 138–39
fruit cordials, 35–36, 186–88, 190–92, 194

garnishes, 74–77
Gimlet, 141
gin cocktails
    Bee's Knees, 126–27
    Bijou, 98–99
    Blackfriar Cocktail, 110–11
    Clover Club, 77, 132–33
    Corpse Reviver No. 2, 70, 142–43

gin cocktails (*continued*)
    Gimlet, 141
    Lord of the Flies, 118–19
    Martinez, 92–93
    Martini, 85
    Meyer LeMon, 166–67
    Montmartre, 112–13
    Negroni, 96–97
    12 Monkeys, 162–63
gins, 18–21
glasses
    drinking, 58
    mixing, 53–54, 61
Greater Antilles, 120–21
guava cordial, 160, 186

habanero tincture, 146, 187
hangover remedies, 10
Hawthorne strainers, 55, 62, 66
highballs, 170–71
Hombre Concombre, 158–59

ice, 10, 59–61
ice blocks, 67–70
Improved Toronto, 108–9
Improved Whiskey Cocktail, 70, 203

infused syrups, 33
infusion techniques, 71

jiggers, 56
juicing techniques, 72–74
julep strainers, 54–55

Kentucky Alexander, 13, 168–69

lavender bitters, Micah's, 126, 183
lengtheners, 72, 139
lime cordial, 141, 187
Lion's Tail, 128–29, 156
liqueurs, 35–36
London dry gins, 18
Lord of the Flies, 118–19

macerated syrups, 33–35, 188
Manhattan, 58, 61, 65, 82–83
Margarita, 14, 136–37
Martinez, 92–93
Martini, 85
McGee, Harold, 33
Mean Old Man, 114–15
measuring cups, 56
Meyer LeMon, 166–67

Meyer lemon confit, 166, 189
Meyer lemon cordial, 166, 190
mezcal cocktails
    Smokey Dokey, 146–47
mezcals, 24–25
Micah's cherry sassafras bitters, 102, 182
Micah's lavender bitters, 126, 183
Micah's orange spice bitters, 106, 184
mixing glasses, 53–54, 61
Montmartre, 112–13
Morgenthaler, Jeffrey, 59
Mr. Potato Head approaches, 14–15, 56, 81
muddlers and muddling, 56, 70

Negroni, 96–97
Nelson County Gentleman, 122–23
New American gins, 21

Old Fashioned, 48, 58, 102–3
Old Tom gins, 19
oleo saccharum, 35, 144
Orange Artichoke, 104–5
orange confit, 146, 191
orange spice bitters, Micah's, 106, 184

Parsons, Brad, 48
passion fruit cordial, 166, 190
paw paw cordial, 152, 190
Paw Paw Daiquiri, 152–53
peaches, macerated, 34, 188
pecan orgeat, 156, 191
peelers, 56
pineapple cordial, 150, 158, 192
Plymouth gins, 20
Prohibition era, 170
proof, 199
pumpkin butter, 154, 193
Punch, 8–9, 12, 144–45

raspberry cordial, 132, 194
rhubarb syrup, 160, 194
rinsing, 70–71
rocks glasses, 58
Rose Hill Ruby, 160–61
rum cocktails
    Airmail, 139
    Ancient Mariner, 156
    Daiquiri, 13, 124–25
    Greater Antilles, 120–21

rum cocktails (*continued*)
    Paw Paw Daiquiri, 152–53
    Punch, 144–45
    Rose Hill Ruby, 160–61
rums, 22
rye whiskey cocktails
    Carpetbagger, 150–51
    Improved Toronto, 108–9
    Manhattan, 82–83
    Nelson County Gentleman, 122–23
    Toronto, 108
    Vieux Carré, 88–89
rye whiskies, 26–27

salted rum caramel, 168, 195
savory, as flavor/cocktail component, 13, 17, 168–69
Sazerac, 48, 70, 94–95
scotch whiskies, 28–29
scotch whisky cocktails
    Mean Old Man, 114–15
    Talking Serpent, 116–17
shakers, cocktail, 53–54, 61
shaking techniques, 14, 61–64, 67
Sidecar, 134–35

simple syrups, 32–33
slings, 9–10
sloe gin, 110–11
Smokey Dokey, 146–47
sour, as flavor/cocktail component, 12–15, 37–49
spirits, 12–15, 16–31, 202
spoons, bar, 54, 196
stirring techniques, 14, 62, 64–67
strainers, 54–55
strawberry cordial, 162, 195
sweeteners, 12–15, 31–36
sweet vermouth, 40–41, 44
syrups
    flavored, 33–35, 180, 185, 194
    simple, 32–33

Talking Serpent, 116–17
tea strainers, 55, 62
techniques, 59–77
tequila cocktails
    Hombre Concombre, 158–59
    Margarita, 14, 136–37
tequilas, 24–25

Thomas, Jerry, 12, 65
tiki cocktails, 22
tools, 53–58
Toronto, 108
Tudor, Frederic, 10
tumblers, 58
12 Monkeys, 162–63

Unwed Sailor, 156–57

vermouths, 41–44

Vieux Carré, 88–89
vinegars, 37
vodka cocktails
    Basil Leaf, 164–65
vodkas, 17

Whiskey Sour, 63, 77, 130–31
whiskies, 26–29
Widow's Kiss, 90–91

Yes, Mr. Washington, 154–55